Creating Form in Clay

Creating Form in Clay

Henry Petterson

Reinhold Book Corporation
New York   Amsterdam   London

"...the smothered incandescence of the kiln in the fabulous heat, baking mineral and chemical treasure on mere clay— to issue in all the hues of the rainbow, all shapes of the imagination, and never yield to time...."

Frank Lloyd Wright
Architectural Record
April 1928

Also by the author (with Ray Gerring): *Exploring with Paint* (Reinhold, 1964).

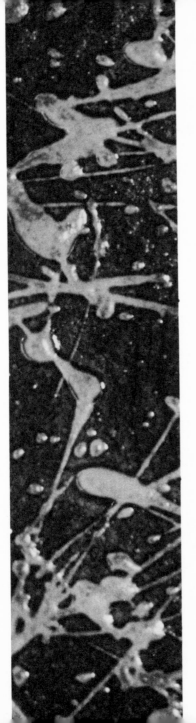

Contents

The Plates

The author is grateful to the many craftsmen who gave permission to reproduce photographs of their work. A partial list of plates is included here. Equally appreciated, however, are the unidentified, generous contributions of the many pupils of the author whose explorations in ceramics helped give this book a wider visual base.

The Craftsmen

Rudy Autio—Fig. I-9, Fig. 9-19
Jerry Baldwin—Fig. 1-14
Rut Bryk—Figs. 1-21—1-23, page 14, Fig. 4-17
Candy Coffelt—Fig. 1-17
John Fassbinder—Fig. 2-13 page 24
Annikka Hovisari—Fig. 1-24
Bob James—Figs. 4-11, 4-12
Taesto Kaasinen—Figs. 3-11—4-21
Donna Lawrence—Fig. 1-15
Phillip Levine—Fig. 3-7, Fig. 12-10
Francesca Lindh—Fig. 1-24
Dave Shaner—Page 52, Fig. 6-6

Lorene Spencer—Figs. 8-18, 8-21
Ralph Spencer—Fig. 2-14
Robert Sperry—Fig. 8-21
James Stipes—Fig. 1-16
Edward Traynor—Figs. 8-12—8-15; Figs. 9-5, 9-7—Pages 70, 75, 76—9-13; Figs. 1-18, 1-19; Figs. 4-18, 4-19; Page 46, Figs. 5-6, 5-7, 5-8, 5-9, 5-10, Figs. 7-9—7-15; Page 88; Fig. 9-17; Fig. 12-12
Wendy Trosper—Figs. 4-14, 4-15
Oiva Toikka—Page 38; Fig. I-11, Fig. 4-20
Mutsuo Yanigihara—Figs. 4-13, 4-16; Figs. 10-6; Page 78; 10-13; Pages 85, 86, 87

Unless otherwise acknowledged, all photographs for this book were taken by the author.

Other Sources of Photographs

Arabia Corporation—Page 32; Fig. 1-23, Page 14; Fig. I-11; Fig. 1-24; Page 38, Fig. 4-21; Fig. 4-17
Interpace Corporation—Figs. 10-10, 10-11, 10-14
Seattle Art Museum—Figs. I-1—I-2, I-6, I-7, I-8; Pages 8, 11
Skutt and Sons—Fig. 11-1

Preface

It is a challenge for any of us to keep fully tuned in to all of the new and unique approaches in any art medium. In the medium of clay, there are many proved ways by which even beginners can achieve reasonable success. It is hoped that the selected processes accompanied by supportive information on the following pages are simple enough, yet sufficiently challenging, to encourage active involvement in working with clay.

Many excellent technical books have been written on this subject, but frequently these are not aimed specifically at the teaching process, the varying abilities of pupils or the special mechanics involved in imaginative instruction. Thus, the information here has been structured particularly to assist those who have the responsibility of solving the special problems of group instruction in working with clay. Exposure to the visual examples and processes explored stimulates fresh ideas.

A survey of clay processes of the past offers some illumination and appreciation of the field. Though so much has happened over the centuries in the development of various methods of working with clay, close parallels between the past and the present exist.

Inspirational visual examples of the work of talented individuals from many cultures are included in this book to illustrate the universality of approaches and methods of working with clay. These one-of-a-kind visual examples are not always defined easily as being clearly the work of professional craftsmen or the unusual and imaginative experiments of highly creative students of the craft. Perhaps this uncertainty in trying to separate the professional from the novice indicates the opportunity and adventure that await all who try their hand with this art medium, however inexperienced or advanced they may be.

There are pros and cons concerning the need to rush in to try the new and the different in all forms of art expression. The "correct answer" cannot be the same for each individual, as we all respond differently to a medium. Thus, in this work an effort has been made to blend the conventional and the past with the exploratory and the new, and to offer traditional visual examples along with uncommon illustrations. This book aims to provide young people and adults with a springboard to clay experiences that are interesting, informative and, above all, enjoyable.

Introduction

With the use of such techniques as the carbon 14 and other age-detection procedures, many discoveries concerning the arts of the past are being made by historians and archeologists. It is no longer hazardous to attempt to pinpoint with some degree of accuracy the date of the earliest examples of man's attempt to use clay in making needed or decorative objects.

As a starting point, it has been confirmed that as early as 18,000 B.C. the simple manipulation of clay was achieved by the peoples living on the European continent, in what is now Czechoslovakia.

It is interesting to speculate how these prehistoric peoples may have learned that clay could be hardened and strengthened by drying through air, or by the sun's heat or fire. Primitive man needed only to find clay exposed to the sun's warmth to discover that this previously damp and crumbly material would take on a hard, dry, dense character. Thus, we can further imagine him contemplating what might happen if the dried clays were placed into or buried in his open fire and allowed to remain until the embers had cooled.

This experimentation into the clay-maturation process led to an important discovery—the vitrification of a previously soft, pliable, inorganic substance. Although it was a primitive method of firing clay, it is still being duplicated most effectively in much the same manner. Civilized man has made some important refinements and improvements in this process, such as the use of electricity or gas as a fuel, to produce the variety and quantity of ceramic items he does today.

To better examine examples of highly developed or fired clay objects, one goes forward in history to approximately 3600 B.C. The illustration of a terra-cotta sculptural figure shown on page 10 is an example of the solid-formed clay process.

It is interesting to note that many of the earliest clay objects were sculptural or modeled in character. Even utilitarian objects seem to have a design quality meant to enhance or complement their functional nature to add a ceremonial feeling.

The Haniwa warrior, a terra-cotta sculpture shown on page 10, presents an excellent example of the multiformed construction found in early ceremonial Japanese clay objects. This particular example dates back to approximately 300 A.D., but was only recently (1930) uncovered in excavations near Tokyo. Sculpture of this type has frequently been found near early Japanese burial sites, and there are indications that it served as a means of protection as well as identification of the grave locations of the departed.

This Haniwa warrior figure stands over 50 inches tall and is particularly significant to us because many of the forming techniques emphasized in this book are to be found in this one sculpture. Applied surface decoration as well as incised pattern abound in the overall surface design of the work. The cylindrical forms that compose the bulky leg structures, the bell-shaped lower body and the supporting base are all a slab-coil-type construction, while the solid-formed technique was used to develop the weapons—sword, bow and arrows. The central figure is hollow, as are the supporting base and the helmeted head.

Terra-cotta as a special clay medium is particularly adapted to sculpture because of its high grog content, which keeps shrinkage at a minimum and thus allows the sculptor freedom to develop large sculptural forms. Although the Haniwa warrior is unglazed, it originally had a decorative paint application that is all but worn away now. It is interest- to note that the tooling techniques shown on the following pages are in many ways similar to those

Head of a Haniwa warrior (pages 10-11).

9

contemporary sculptors and potters use today. The tool marks and the applied-clay technique contribute to make the Haniwa warrior seem much less than 1,600 years old, as the detailed photographs clearly indicate.

Terra-cotta sculpture is treated in a much different manner in Fig. 1-6 on page 12 by Alexander Archipenko (1887-1963), the Russian-born American sculptor who utilized terra-cotta in many of his better-known works. Archipenko developed a unique surface treatment on his terra-cotta figures. By rubbing the surfaces with a rough carborundum stone, a highly polished nonfire surface glaze was developed. Often it was so highly polished that it was very difficult to distinguish from a transparent glaze. *The Bride* (1936) is graphic evidence of this kind of clear nonkiln glaze, which is possible to achieve by rubbing and burnishing fired clay with abrasive stones. Continuous hand rubbing of a fired-clay surface can produce such a patina.

Fig. I-2 The Haniwa warrior is perhaps the most famous clay sculptural figure of our examples; it stands over 50″ high and shows some evidence of the surface-paint designing technique. The piece is interesting because of the many different clay-forming techniques used in it.

Fig. I-1 This solid-formed terra-cotta sculptural figure of a mourner is attributed to Egypt's predynastic era, about 3600 B.C. The heavily grogged surface suggests that even at this early date craftsmen were fully aware of the shrinkage problem in construction and modeling with clay.

Fig. I-4   This detailed photograph presents another view of the Haniwa warrior's back, emphasizing the coiled belt and weapons. The surface detail is consistent with the overall size of the work and does not dominate or diminish the main body design.

Fig. I-5   This back-of-the-helmet view of the Haniwa warrior illustrates several distinctive surface-design techniques: applied relief with small clay rivets, a sgraffito line design and a surface-scratched texture.

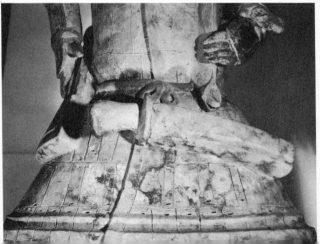

Fig. I-3   The lower-body detail of the Haniwa warrior demonstrates the solid-formed process used to fashion the weapons and the hands. The overall body surface carries a combed, or scored, design, perhaps the result of the artist's unique tools.

Fig. I-6 Alexander Archipenko's *The Bride*, made of terra-cotta in 1936, has a highly polished nonkiln-glazed surface. On close examination the heavy grog content adds an interesting textural facet to the work and points out the importance clay sculptors have placed in this element of the material's composition.

Fig. I-7 *The Warrior*, a hollow earthenware figure attributed to the Tarascan culture of Mexico (1200 A.D.), provides an excellent example of an early nonglaze surface-decoration technique. The vertical stripes were painted on, but in the course of time have almost completely disappeared.

Fig. I-8 This small earthenware figure fragment, no more than 3″ tall, was found on the Gulf coast of Mexico and dates back to pre-Columbian times (900 A.D.). The solid- and slab-formed processes are evident in this work, as is pressed-relief surface design.

Fig. I-9 A 20th Century sculptural clay figure, by Rudy Autio, demonstrates the robust character of the abstract expressionist school of ceramics. Note the heavy tooling and the informal glaze-application technique.

The figure of a warrior on page 12 is an earthenware (low-fire) clay sculpture which also utilized a nonglaze decoration on the surface. Surface designs were frequently painted on, but the pigments have deteriorated with time. The abstract expressionist ceramic torso by Rudy Autio on page 12 is a combination of bare slab and glaze surface treatment.

Although the range and diversity of approaches used in the past exhibit a great degree of variety, so many strong similarities exist with the present that perhaps ceramics, as an art form, has not been able to free itself to expand upon its strong traditions. Present-day craftsmen are beginning to venture further and perhaps future craftsmen, imaginative pupils, will do much to help lead the way.

Glossary terms: Carbon 14, sculptural, Haniwa, terra-cotta, nonfire glaze.

Fig. I-10 Contemporary sculptors find clay an excellent medium. This interesting figure contrasts heavy textural surface modeling with white matte glaze. The detail at the right shows a variety of surface techniques: sgraffito, applied relief and cutout areas.

1. Flat-Slab-Formed Shapes

f any process in this book is to be singled out as he preferred beginning experience for pupils, it nust be the flat-slab form. First, the slab form can readily serve as a sampler, both in developing surace-tooling techniques and in glazing exploration. The limiting factor in the simple slab experience is hat very little of the fabrication or construction experience of other forms is involved. Perhaps this s an advantage for the pupil, since an initial experience in working with clay should not be so nvolved as to overwhelm the student with complex construction techniques.

The examples (Figs. 1-1 and 1-2) being prepared on page 16 show several approaches to developing he slab form. A large, flat slab of clay is first prepared by rolling, throwing or pressing. The pupil may choose an outline contour that is rectangular, round, a combination of forms, or even a shape hat has a representational characteristic, such as hose shown on pages 20 and 21. When the student has selected the outside dimensions and outlined his slab, he can trim the excess away and begin the surface designing directly. If the slab is rectangular, the experience may include breaking up the total space in a gridlike fashion and then ooling each enclosed segment with a different design or texture.

A pressed or rolled surface design may be attempted in a part of the rectangle. The student design on page 19 was produced by carving first nto soft cork, then transferring the design to a freshly prepared slab. It should be noted that the finished design is in reverse and that the previously deep or carved areas in the cork then become raised-relief segments of the final design.

The example (Fig. 1-18) on page 21 shows a slab

form that is much less defined; it is quite informal and robust. No carefully drawn contour or shape was attempted. Only the hands were used as a tool to press the slab into the desired shape. A quick brushing of glaze over part of the piece added another facet of surface contrast and change. The finished piece is held upright and supported with a dowel, or rod, extending from the block of wood several inches into the slab (page 21). The hole into which the dowel fits was pushed into the clay early, before it dried.

The examples shown on page 23 are considerably more structured, or planned. The lion figure is particularly interesting in that a combination of surface-design techniques was used. Note the pressed-relief; the sgraffito, or carved line, technique; and the applied-relief shapes, all in one work. Another example of combining several surface-design techniques in a single work is found on page 21.

In most of the flat-slab examples, including commercially prepared tiles, some special stabilizing treatment of the back of the piece should be used. Clay warpage is frequently a problem, since flat slabs tend to dry unevenly. There are several methods of preventing slab warpage. One is to carve troughs or grooves into the back surface of a slab, as shown on page 17. Also, the problem of warpage is often aggravated by one side of the slab drying at a different rate than the other. To equalize the drying, frequent turning of the slabs can help diminish the warpage. Sandwiching a slab of clay between two flat plaster bats also tends to allow moisture absorption that is equal on both surfaces.

In the pupil's effort to design a slab, many more tools may be utilized than perhaps in any other

Complex shapes, textures and glaze colors are placed toether in this mosaic of individual flat-slab shapes.

single process. None, however, may be more effective or sensitive than one's own fingertips.

The flat-slab form allows, and usually encourages, the pupil's use of more than one glaze. The glazing pattern or design of a slab project is often simplified for the pupil, since rounded deep contours and curved surfaces are not usually encountered. Thus, glazes may be brushed on quite easily by the beginner. To intensify the pupil's interest, a variety of glazes should be made available for the process of decorating flat slabs.

As a beginning exploration in clay, the flat-slab-formed process is particularly recommended, as it provides even younger pupils with valuable experience in surface design and decoration that will be most useful in all of the processes encountered in this book.

Glossary terms: Flat slab, pressed relief, sgraffito, applied relief.

SUGGESTED TOOLS AND MATERIALS FOR THE FLAT-SLAB-FORMED PROCESS

Clay (grogged)
Canvas work panels
Kitchen knife
A variety of surface-decorating tools and objects
Glaze brushes
Glaze
Plaster drying slabs (optional)

Fig. 1-1   A rectangular shape is being cut from the prepared slab of clay. Flat-slab shapes may have a variety of contours: round, oval or, perhaps, subject-oriented. The clay is ½″ thick and quite pliable at this stage.

Fig. 1-2   The pupil is designing the surface of a rectangular shape. The ridges on a screwdriver handle make a distinctive repeat pattern. This particular approach involves the breakup of space into irregular shapes, with a different texture applied in each area.

16

Fig. 1-3   On the left is the stylized design of a round shape. The finished rectangular shape at right is being tooled on the back to prevent warpage of the tile. A bent wire works well as the groove-cutting tool.

Figs. 1-4, 5   These two fired flat-slab shapes show the back-tooling treatment. The grooves may be carved in either direction, depending upon the surface design. It is preferable to run the grooves on the back, counter to the lines of the front design.

Fig. 1-6   This view of the back-tooling of the round, flat slab shows three nibs, or raised areas, being squeezed from the moist clay. One nib has had a hole pierced through it to accommodate a hanging cord; the other two help keep the work balanced, whether hanging or displayed flat.

Fig. 1-7   A tooled surface design often may be softened or altered by pressing or, as in this case, by rolling. Careful control of the rolling pin will blend harsh areas into a subtle composition.

17

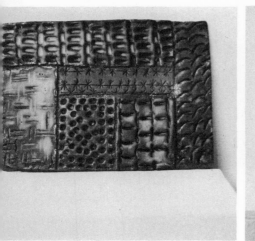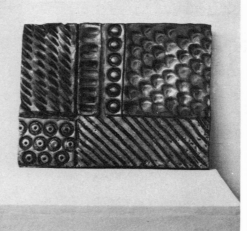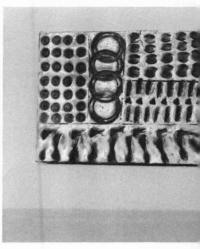

Figs. 1-8—1-12 These exploratory flat-slab shapes show a variety of textural treatments. Many simple tools have been used to change the surface of the clay. In most instances, such slab shapes offer a good opportunity to try out glaze combinations. These texture and glaze samplers allow pupils to experiment widely and thereby perhaps avoid ruining future works with improper glaze combinations.

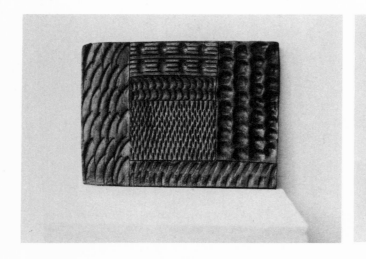

Fig. 1-13 A pressed-relief design is shown in this slab shape. First, a design is carved into a semirigid surface such as cork, plaster, styrofoam or wood. Then, by pressing this plate into a moist slab of clay, an impression in reverse is made. A pressed-relief slab design takes glaze well, allowing the high ridges to stand out.

Fig. 1-14 An abstract arrangement of shapes appears in this pressed-slab design. Glaze is used sparingly, thus allowing the clay's inherent surface texture to dominate the work.

Fig. 1-15 This striking composition shows both the line design of the carved cork plate and the texture of the canvas-covered work surface. A single semimatte glaze draws attention to the high ridges of the work.

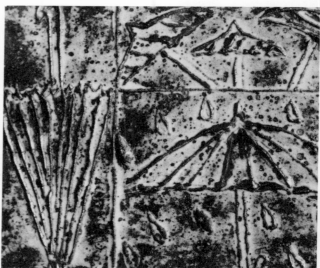

Fig. 1-16 A smooth cork-cut plate was pressed into a clay slab to achieve this glazed relief composition. Extremely high firing produced the mottled surface texture by burning away portions of the white glaze. Note that the high ridges are first to burn away to the clay-body color.

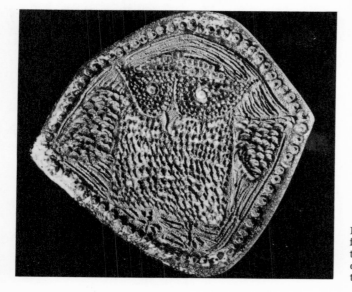

Fig. 1-17 The subject matter often suggests the outline of a flat-slab shape. This highly textured bird is designed to fill the free form generally, yet the interior design suggests a direction or outline. Partial glazing highlights portions of the work.

Fig. 1-18 A flat-slab shape may take on a sculptural quality, as it has in this hand-pressed informal composition. Glaze and inscription join to make the face of this work interesting.

Fig. 1-19 The back side of the same work is left unglazed. The square, heavy-grained, charcoal-brushed block supports the slab by means of the insertion of a dowel into an impression made when the clay was still wet.

Fig. 1-21 An intricate surface design makes this flat-slab piece distinctive. Cutout areas add still another design element. Although the outline shape is simple, it helps convey the message intended.

Fig. 1-20 This flat sculptural slab was constructed with two distinct surface-design methods. The raised portions were achieved by a pressed-relief process and by the paddling of applied clay to a semi-flat state. Sgraffito, tooling and partial glazing complete the work.

21

Fig. 1-22 The flat-slab process in clay is often closely related to the painting process: glaze is applied in a painterly fashion in this work. Many tile designers use a full palette of glaze colors to achieve the desired combination of tones.

Fig. 1-23 A variety of surface-design techniques appears in this decorative slab shape. Interesting clay buttons and a cloisonné treatment that outlines glazed areas dominate the work. Note that the simple, strong outline shape contrasts with the delicate interior design.

Fig. 1-24 This tile wall demonstrates how variety can be achieved with a single design element, the circle. The various sizes of the circles, the brilliant glaze colors and the change of pace in placement contribute to make this flat slab a clay work of both utility and beauty.

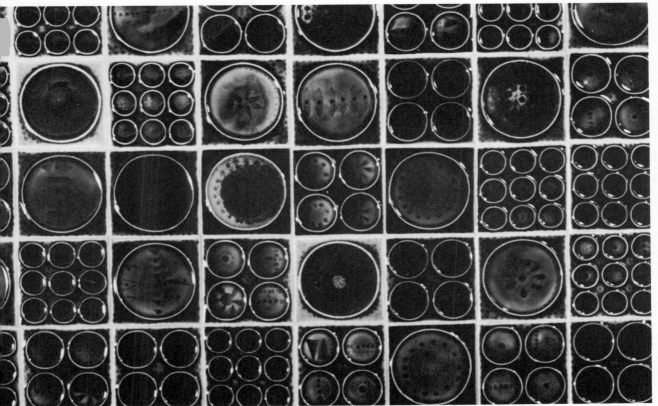

The head shape of this large figure vessel is removable. The white matte surface glaze is scratched through in a sgraffito manner.

2. Slab-Coil-Formed Shapes

The coil process of forming in clay was one of the earliest methods developed by man. In our slab adaption, we borrow heavily from this long tradition of coiling to make cylinders. Throughout the world, versions of the slab-coil method are still being used to produce large pots, particularly in remote villages of Japan and by the *olla* (water cask) makers in Mexico.

The main advantage of working in the slab-coil process is that an object can be built in a relatively short time. One can also be relatively spontaneous in constructing a variety of clay shapes with the slab-coil method.

We will concentrate on constructing a wind bell, which can be conical or cylindrical in shape. The eventual ring, or tone, of a wind bell is diminished by extreme changes in surface thickness and ridges, so the fewer coils used, the better.

First, the throat, or opening dimension, of the bell is determined. A disc, or circle, of clay is cut from the corner of a ½"-thick slab (Fig. 2-1). At the same time, the eyelet holder for the bell clapper is fashioned from a thin coil of clay. This eyelet is pressed and tooled securely into the prepared clay disc (Fig. 2-2).

The next step is to cut and apply the flat strips of clay from the same prepared slab. To simplify construction and to minimize the joints, the strips of clay may be increased to any width that can be handled conveniently by the student.

The first slab coil is curled around the top of the disc and firmly pressed together with an overlap joint. The initial coil should be joined to the disc with firm tooling on the inside, since this will be the roof of the bell. The joint on the outside should be pressed together thoroughly as well. The suc-

ceeding coils are attached similarly. To prevent vertical cracks occurring between coils, it is advisable that each succeeding coil joint be positioned alternately from the previous coil. This staggering of joined coils will ultimately help strengthen the finished work.

After the desired height of the wind bell has been achieved (at least 3"), it is inverted on the work board. The bottom disc now becomes the top of the bell. An attached holder for the bell may be fashioned from the same clay, pressed and tooled into place at the center of the disc. An alternate method is to squeeze a holder from the top disc, as shown in the example on page 29. To accommodate a hanging cord, pierce a hole through the holder while the clay is still plastic.

Finishing of the bell's exterior surface may be accomplished in many ways. For a clean, straight-sided finish, use a heavy sandpaper block to remove indentations and ridges. The bottom lip can be leveled by turning the bell carefully on a piece of sandpaper. Finish tooling is best accomplished when the bell is at the leather-hard stage. Major surface tooling or designing should be attempted only while the clay is still pliable and not so brittle as to crack from the pressure of tooling or handling.

The wind bell's clapper may now be cut from the same slab and fitted approximately to the finished inside opening of the bell. After drying, further sanding and tooling of the clapper are necessary to give it proper clearance and swing inside the bell. This clearance should allow a minimum of ⅜" between clapper and bell. It is important to prepare the clapper with two small holes, one at top and bottom, to accommodate the tie twines.

After bisque firing, the bell may be glazed on its

exterior or may be left unglazed. (The clapper need not be glazed.) Dry footing, or nonglazing, of the rim of a bell is a distinct advantage if glaze is applied. Kiln stacking is a problem if bells are glazed without this dry footing precaution.

The final assembly of the bell includes hanging the clapper from the eyelet at the top of the bell. If the bell is deep, maneuvering the tie twine might prove difficult. By using a bent wire, the string can be looped through the eyelet and pulled back through, much as one would thread the head of a needle. The clapper is positioned no more than ½" or so inside the bell to insure a satisfactory ring.

The wind bell now needs an important addition to make it function properly. A wind sail, or flap, is required and should be attached 3" or 4" from the bottom of the clapper. Without this wind sail, the bell cannot ring. The wind sail may be fashioned from thin metal, plastic or cardboard. It is important that the twine or string used in tying together individual parts of a wind bell be braided, as is fishline. This is suggested since the twirling of the wind sail will cause any unbraided twine to un-

ravel. Oiled heavy-leather lacing makes an attractive and strong outdoor hanging line for the bell.

The wind bell is one item that adapts well to the slab-coil method of construction. Bowls, branch bottles and sculptural figure shapes can also be effectively constructed through this process.

Glossary terms: Slab coil, wind bell, dry-footing, bell clapper, bisque, branch bottle.

SUGGESTED TOOLS AND MATERIALS FOR THE SLAB-COIL-FORMED PROCESS

Clay
Clay work panels
Cutting knife
Modeling tools
Sandpaper block
Glaze (optional)
Cardboard, thin plastic or metal
Braided twine or fishline
Oiled leather lacing

Fig. 2-1 After the pupil has prepared a slab of clay, he cuts a base shape for his slab-coil cylinder in the form of a disc. This is done near the edge of the slab so that the main slab body remains intact.

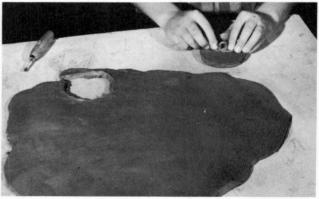

Fig. 2-2 The base disc is lifted away as shown; then a small coil of clay is fashioned into a loop and pressed firmly into the disc. This eyelet will serve an important function in this work—a clay wind bell.

Fig. 2-3 The remaining clay slab is cut into strips that will be coiled around the base disc in a repeating fashion. It is important to press each coil firmly into the succeeding one so that the joints will remain together.

Fig. 2-4 After the cylinder has reached the desired height, the pupil may continue pressing together the joints, smoothing lumps and protruding clay areas. Each slab coil should be joined to the preceding coil at a different location to strengthen the cylinder shape.

Fig. 2-5 A bell shape becomes more recognizable when a holder is applied. Note that the cylinder has been turned upside down: the bottom disc now becomes the top of the bell shape. The clay is most pliable and plastic at this stage; thus, the holder may be joined readily to the cylinder by pressing and squeezing.

Fig. 2-6 The bell has now been glazed. The holder is strengthened by the surrounding glaze. An application of wax-resist was given the footing, making the glaze firing simpler. Note that the glaze has a tendency to sag or run, yet is retained at the resist-applied border.

Fig. 2-7 These three wind bells were constructed with the slab-coil method. The bell on the left is only partially glazed, allowing the inherent iron and grog in the clay body to dominate the surface texture and color. The fully glazed example on the right has a squeezed holder, rather than one that is applied.

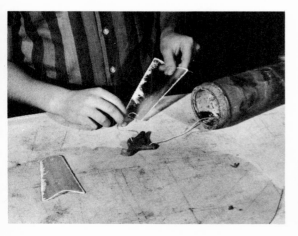

Fig. 2-8 To function properly, a wind bell needs a clapper and a wind sail. Here the pupil is attaching all the parts to be strung to the interior loop, prepared during construction. A cardboard shape or, as pictured, a wind sail may be cut from corrugated plastic sheathing. Braided fishline works well as the tie string.

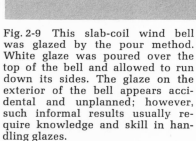

Fig. 2-9 This slab-coil wind bell was glazed by the pour method. White glaze was poured over the top of the bell and allowed to run down its sides. The glaze on the exterior of the bell appears accidental and unplanned; however, such informal results usually require knowledge and skill in handling glazes.

Fig. 2-10 Wind bells may be decorated in other ways as well as with glaze. Here, a thin coil of clay is attached in a spiral fashion to give the surface an applied dimension.

Fig. 2-11 Two entirely different types of wind bells are shown here. The bell on the right utilizes curved discs of clay, spaced on a hanging cord. Wind movement causes the small clay balls to strike the discs, resulting in an interesting sound. The bell on the left is composed of hanging strips of clay that strike each other through wind movement.

Fig. 2-12 This vessel is an example of the slab-coil process. Careful joining and sanding of the coil-constructed body have resulted in a smooth surface. Notice how limited glazing gives the piece variety.

Fig. 2-13 The slab-coil process lends itself to sculptural shapes well. This tall figure has an applied-clay surface design, paddled and flattened to conform to the main body form.

Fig. 2-14 This coil-constructed container stands over 24″ tall. The exterior surface tooling involved a vertical skiving of the clay. No attempt has been made to remove the tool marks; the excess interior-glaze drippings were allowed to remain on the exterior lip.

In this many-figured single composition, the heavily textured surface and a single glaze color unify the impact.

3. Hand-Formed Shapes

The hand forming of clay is related closely to the pinch-pot method. However, it can invite much more than the making of pots. For our illustrations, hand forming is used in a modeling or sculptural sense. A basic shape is first determined, after which the clay is worked by the student into the hollow of the hand (page 34). These round bowl shapes can be made in any size and then attached to other similar shapes to form bodies, heads, necks or other parts of a sculptural work.

As shown in the example on pages 34-35, several hand-formed shapes are combined to develop the head and neck shape of a fisherman. The bird on page 36 is an example of a single hand-formed shape being used. For the most part, the examples shown are all hollow, with the wall thickness limited to less than 1″. The hand-formed shapes as a sculptural method offer the student little restriction in the joining process, since the surface texture is robust, less defined and characterized by overlapping planes.

In the hand-forming method, the clay is in the wet and plastic state. This is necessary to impart a sense of spontaneity to the work. Fig. 3-8 on page 36 is an example of the wet hand-forming process that utilizes an added or applied-design element. These strips of clay are attached over the hollow body shape and pressed into the adjoining clay, all while the clay is in a damp, plastic state.

As a variation, the applied hat shape of the fisherman is shaped from a slab of the same clay, then pressed over the head. The tie straps, or hat strings, made of clay are also pressed into and over the original form during this initial operation. The facial features—eyes, nose, chin and mustache—are all squeezed from the clay of the original head

form. If this kind of surface treatment is attempted, it is important that the depth of the clay body walls be fairly thick. At least ¾″ should be allowed so that the trimming and "borrowing" of clay does not result in very thin spaces in the finished work. Since hand-formed shapes often have a variance in wall thickness, it is important that the drying not be done hastily. This slow maturation will allow the various thicknesses to dry uniformly. As a further rule, the larger the piece, the more caution needs to be taken in the drying and maturing. Still another consideration is to give the finished work a slower first, or bisque, firing to help diminish the possibility of fractures.

If small cracks do develop in such a sculptural work and are objectionable in a design sense, then an applied glaze may be used to fill in these cracks. If glazing is not applicable or desired, a colored epoxy cement mixture may be pressed into cracks to diminish such defects. For some pieces, such defects are best left unaltered and are allowed to remain as part of the character of the finished work.

Clay sculptors in the past have developed several unique methods of eliminating the necessity of hollow coring, or gouging out of the center of a work. It is not uncommon to find head shapes that have been made of solid clay, some 6″ thick or more. The method used by sculptors to avoid failures in firing is to pierce such a solid mass of clay with a long, thin needle or hatpin. By allowing these minute hollow shafts to be placed through the work, the heavy clay pockets are eliminated. With most sculptural work such piercings would not be noticeable and definitely would help ensure against kiln mishaps. Still another consideration when working with a solid mass of clay is to be sure that the clay is strongly grogged and compounded from a clay body that is known to be as low in the shrinkage factor as possible.

The glazing or nonglazing of hand-formed clay pieces, as with all work, is a matter of personal taste. However, it is frequently most effective to allow sculptural work to remain unglazed, as the roughness of the surface texture of a sculptural work can become competitive or conflict with an application of glaze. Partial glazing could provide an acceptable alternative if glaze is justified in enhancing a particular work.

Glossary terms: Pinch pot, applied design, fracture, epoxy cement.

SUGGESTED TOOLS AND MATERIALS FOR THE HAND-FORMED PROCESS

Clay (heavily grogged)
Canvas work panel
Modeling tools (optional)
Thin plastic (to retain drying)
Piercing needle (for solid clay)

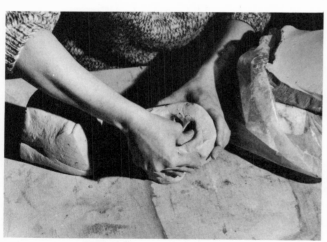

Fig. 3-1 A handful of clay is shaped into a ball; then the center is pushed in, forming a hollow shape.

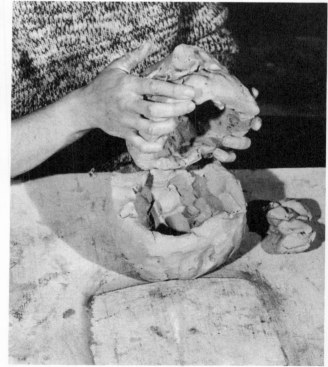

Fig. 3-2 Two similarly fashioned hollow shapes are joined to form a head. The clay is quite pliable at this stage, and may be joined by pressing and squeezing.

34

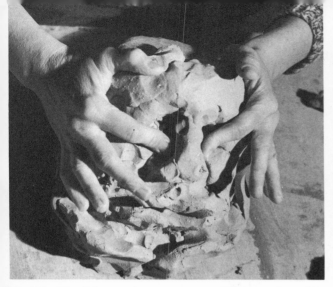

Fig. 3-3   The fisherman's nose, eyes and lips are shaped by adding clay to the exterior of the original head shape. Only a general likeness is sought for at this stage; detail will be added later.

Fig. 3-4   A hat is fashioned from a large slab, then draped and pressed over the head.

Fig. 3-5   Detail is added to the overall shape by pressing and squeezing the clay where needed. Refining is omitted, allowing the work to retain its robust quality.

Fig. 3-6   A variation of the hand-forming method is shown in this wall mask. Flat and hollowed out in the back, the work is modeled in a rough sculptural manner.

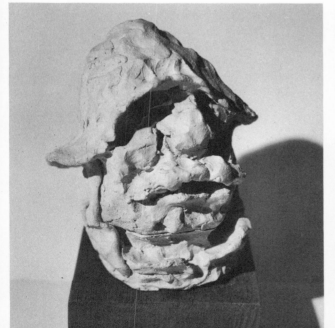

Fig. 3-7 This sculptural figure shows the combination of refinement of features and a rough body-surface texture. A glaze covers all but the face and hands.

Fig. 3-8 The use of applied strips of clay adds a heavy textural treatment and ties together segments of this figure structurally.

Fig. 3-9 This hand-formed bird shape is almost entirely closed, with only a small hole on the underside leading to the hollow center. The piece was partially dipped into glaze.

Fig. 3-10 These round bird forms are hollow and have pressed-relief facial features, with partial glazing applied over a heavily grogged clay body.

The sides of this squared horse are treated individually with line, texture and color.

4. Box-Formed Shapes

There are a number of ways to design a box shape with clay. The shape may be square, or long and narrow, or it might even have bowed or curved sides, as shown in Figs. 4-18 and 4-19. The corners may be sharp and clean or may be fashioned together in a much more informal manner, allowing overlapping and tool marks to remain.

The construction technique for each of these methods may vary widely, depending on a pupil's dexterity and the consistency of the clay. For instance, in a step-by-step sequence, the top, bottom and sides of the box are precut according to a predetermined cardboard cutout, or template. After cutting around this template, certain portions of the slab are cut away to facilitate assembling the box. The clay is allowed to cure and dry for one day into a semistiff state. The assembly of the box involves folding up the adjoining sides and literally pressing and gluing the slabs together.

There is a more direct method, one which eliminates the drying period by tool-pressing the damp sides together in one operation. This approach can prove unpredictable, however, since handling of the moist clay in box-building invites the risk of collapse or distortion. By allowing the individual slabs to dry and stiffen, there is apt to be much less opportunity for a box to become misshapen through handling.

For larger box shapes it is strongly recommended that the clay slabs be stiffened first. With smaller clay boxes this is not as critical, because there is less span between walls and less distortion develops.

If surface tooling or designing is to be done using the wet-clay, or direct, method, it is best to avoid tooling the individual slab shapes before assembling them into place. This is important, since the applied design will tend to lose its clarity during the building process. The nonstiffened clay sides will allow surface carving or designing after being assembled and partially dried. Press or relief design is not advised with dry or stiffened clay as the pressure is apt to pull apart or split the sides of the box.

One advantage in working with wet-clay slabs is that the sides of the box being constructed need not be an exact fit. The clay, being pliable, allows the pupil freedom to bend or push the walls into the general shape desired. Excess clay or overlaps may be sliced away after the assembling. However, prestiffened slabs need to be measured or cut very accurately, then joined with care.

In both the wet and the prestiffened methods, the finishing of joints may vary considerably. Smooth, sharp corners such as those found in the example in Fig. 4-12 give the box a clean geometric appearance, while the example in Fig. 4-15 has softer corners and is less formal. Even the tool and finger marks are left on this box as part of its structural and surface design.

As with all clay construction, the wet-clay box will tend to shrink considerably through drying and firing, sometimes as much as 15 to 20 per cent of its original wet size. The prestiffened method, on the other hand, will not allow as much shrinkage and distortion.

Pupils may wish to consider the sketch or plan sheet method mentioned earlier, as shown in Fig. 4-1. The template is made from thin cardboard or ticket board and can be folded into a box much the same size as the intended finished work (Fig. 4-2). This cardboard guide allows the pupil to familiarize himself with proportion, as well as with the construction method to be used. The template laid on top of the clay slab acts as an outline and permits scoring the individual parts before assembly (Fig. 4-3).

It is important for the pupil to take into account the overlaps necessary in putting the box together and to anticipate the slab's thickness, which will differ from that of the paper template. Accuracy on adhering strictly to this outline is not so critical as it seems, since pliable clay will stretch and bend to meet and conform to a degree.

To facilitate construction, a simple corner support cut from a cardboard box, as shown in Fig. 4-4, can be fashioned to help students in their efforts to square the box corners as they work. By placing the partially constructed clay box in this simple supportive device and pressing the walls and corners firmly against the sides (Fig. 4-5), the pupil can true his box and minimize distortion. If the box corners have been cut reasonably square, the corner support works well (Figs. 4-6–4-8). If not, the joints may be forced open by pressure in the corner-supporting device. A wooden paddle or flat block may be used lightly to pat the clay box into shape. When the box assembly is completed and has dried to a leather-hard state, sanding and scraping may be attempted to further define the box shape (Fig. 4-9).

A variation of the process is seen in Fig. 4-13. Here a relief technique of glaze stripes was applied to change the surface design of the completed

Fig. 4-1 The pupil is laying out a box shape on heavy tagboard. This template design assists him in visualizing the box-construction process before attempting the work in clay.

Fig. 4-2 The tagboard template is cut, creased and folded to form the box. This preliminary exercise is invaluable for pupils who have had little experience in the design and fabrication of such works.

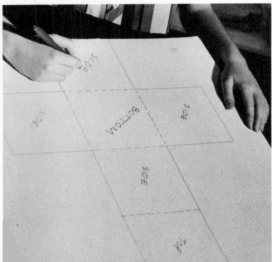

Fig. 4-3 The template serves to outline the general shapes needed in this box construction. After defining the bottom (1), the sides (2, 3, 4 and 5) and the top (6), further creasing and cutting may be made directly in the clay.

Fig. 4-4 The individual parts of the box are folded together, one at a time. Cross-tooling of the joints throughly ensures that the finished box will hold together. Note the corner support, covered with a rough-surfaced canvas.

Fig. 4-5 When the sides and bottom are assembled, the pupil begins to get the feel of the box shape. The corners are pressed firmly together.

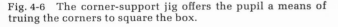

Fig. 4-6 The corner-support jig offers the pupil a means of truing the corners to square the box.

work. Further variations can be achieved by combining other forms with the basic box shape (Figs. 4-17, 4-20—4-21), by using the sgraffito technique (Figs. 4-10, 4-14) and by imaginative glazing (Figs. 4-11, 4-16).

The box-formed process is unique because, traditionally, clay has been worked in the round, with a minimum of joints and corners. Pupils who excel at geometric exercises or in similar types of constructions should do well in clay-box designing.

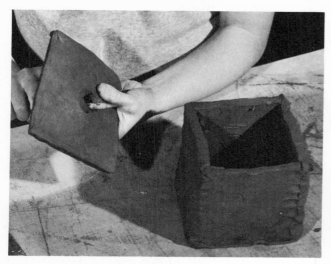

Fig. 4-7 The top of the box is ready to be attached. The student prepares an opening by pushing a pencil through from the bottom, or inside, of the lid.

Fig. 4-8 The top of the box is now secured. When pressed firmly from all sides, the joints tend to weld together, minimizing cracks.

Fig. 4-9 A hacksaw blade is used to scrape excess clay from the high areas of the box. Valleys and high ridges disappear during this leveling process.

Fig. 4-10 A scratched, or sgraffito, design may be applied to a box. A sharp nail serves well as a design tool at this leather-hard stage.

Fig. 4-11 Each side of this box shape has its own glaze design. The highly textured clay body offers an excellent contrast to the individual designs.

Fig. 4-12 The applied-glaze design leads the eye from one side of this box to the other. The true corners demonstrate the skill necessary in developing geometric shapes from clay.

Glossary terms: Template, relief design, prestiffened, distortion, corner support, true.

SUGGESTED TOOLS AND MATERIALS FOR THE BOX-FORMED PROCESS

Clay
Canvas work panels
Clay-cutting knife
Thin cardboard (for template)
Clay paddle
Sandpaper
Corner support

Fig. 4-13 A multiform box face is designed with alternating glazed and bare clay stripes. The glazed stripes lie slightly below the upper surface of the clay and are surprisingly uniform. This effect is achieved by overall glazing and selective scraping.

Fig. 4-14   This box shape is heavily designed, with a sgraffito-textured surface. Corners are beveled to soften the severity of the work.

Fig. 4-15   Several surface-decoration techniques appear in this long, narrow box shape. Note the combed design and pressed-relief combination.

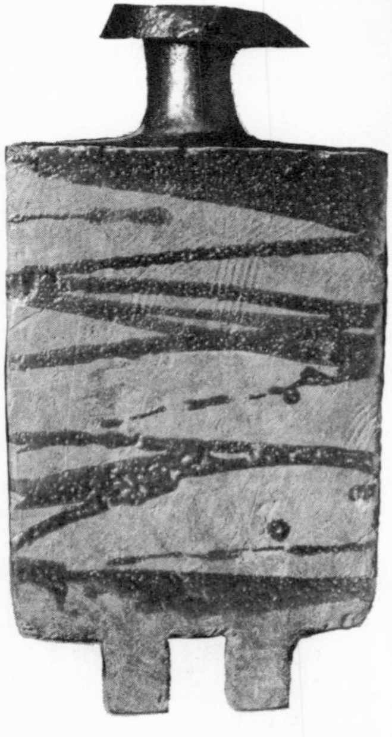

Fig. 4-16   The footing of this piece is strong; it extends the length of the work, elevating the box to achieve a lighter sense of proportion. Note the contrast of minimal glazing with the bare clay surface.

Fig. 4-17   This complex and extensive collection of box shapes is combined uniquely with a wide array of colorful tiles and glaze treatments.

Figs. 4-18—4-19 Long, narrow box shapes with curved sides offer a change of pace from traditionally shaped works.

The top view of the same box shows the opening detail, glaze application and edge beveling.

Fig. 4-20 This horse combines a clay box with cylindrical shapes. Note the interesting sgraffito addition of a rider.

Fig. 4-21 Box shapes are frequently used as abstract body forms for figures and animals. This ceramic horse-and-knight piece features an applied-relief design as well as a white glaze.

5. Collage-Formed Shapes

The collage-slab process can be described as the pasting of overlapping strips of clay into a flat composition. Variety and contrast are obtained through an interesting use of different clay and grog textures. Students should again consider strongly grogged clay bodies as a precaution to help avoid the stress of shrinkage found in the flat, interwoven structure. In maturing a clay collage, the drying from the wet state to leather-hard and beyond to the firing is the critical factor.

The slabs of variously colored and textured clay are prepared as shown on page 48. These slabs are formed from a *single* clay body. The three slabs are flattened on canvas-covered work panels at the same time. The slabs are approximately ½" thick and may vary in diameter from 6" to as much as 24", depending on the size of the pupil's proposed work.

It is usually best if the pupil has a plan for his collage composition in mind before proceeding. A quick way to develop such a plan is to experiment by constructing a trial segment of the collage. With such a sampler the pupil may better determine if his finished composition will hold together and be properly proportioned.

Other students may find it more adventurous to work directly and spontaneously with the collage-slab process, and they should be encouraged to do so.

It is advantageous to work with a medium-firm clay, or see that the clay slab has a setting-up period, uncovered, of several hours. The collage itself should be covered loosely with a thin plastic sheeting during the finishing period. This slow maturation of the collage will permit slow stiffening, which is critical for this kind of slab project. To facilitate

cutting and placement, the necessary tools for the collage clay process should be readily at hand. These tools need be few in number and might consist of merely a wooden clay-modeling tool with a cutter edge or a common kitchen knife.

Strips and shapes of clay are cut from the previously large slabs of clay and placed to interlock and overlap according to the pupil's idea of the pattern or design. The collage construction proceeds directly on the canvas clay board with only the back side of the design being exposed during the process (Fig. 5-3).

The pressure necessary to apply the clay strips with one's fingers can be determined with a little practice. Too light a pressure will not allow the clay strips to adhere to each other properly, or wide gaps may develop, thus keeping the design from holding together properly. A too-heavy pressure will cause an overflattening of the clay on the finish side by forcing or pressing deeply into the adjoining clay strips and will tend to obliterate the design.

In most instances, the overall thickness of the collage strips should vary between ⅜" to ⅝". Extreme variance in thickness, gaps or openings throughout portions of the composition should be avoided, since these uneven areas create structural stress and cracks or open breaks often appear. It is recommended that for several days after the collage composition has been completed a loose coating of thin plastic garment covers be laid loosely over the finished work. The drying is done at normal room temperature. Direct sunlight or drying outdoors should be avoided in all collage techniques, since the combination of air and heat encourages a sudden loss of moisture from the clay

This large clay collage is over 24" square. The clay strips were applied horizontally as well as vertically.

and strains the composition. In drying the work it is important that both sides, top and bottom of the collage have an opportunity to dry as equally as possible. Transferring or turning the work can be accomplished by providing two dry canvas work panels, one on the top, one on the bottom of the work, much like a sandwich. To admit air circulation equally to top and bottom, rotation of the composition from one panel to the other can be made, allowing surface drying for one side and then the other side. The final preparatory step, transferring the finished collage slab to the kiln, can be accomplished best by carefully sliding the work from the canvas panel directly onto the kiln shelf. This is the preferred approach, whether a front-loading or top-loading kiln is used. For a particularly large collage, transferring can be accomplished by carefully placing the kiln shelf on top of the work and then turning it over and removing the canvas panel. The same

procedures for firing described in Chapter 11 should prevail when the collage-slab project is fired. Since the collage is usually free from the problems of gas pockets, it is possible to apply glaze before the initial firing. Glazing the collage is frequently no necessary because of the many surface changes in planes and colors in the collage.

The photographs on pages 49 and 50 offer various treatments of the collage-formed process.

Glossary terms: Collage, clay strips, transferring

SUGGESTED TOOLS AND MATERIALS FOR THE COLLAGE-FORMED PROCESS

Clay (use single clay body with color variation)
Clay work panels (one for each color clay)
Grog (to vary texture)
Kitchen knife

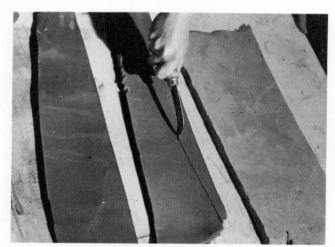

Fig. 5-1　A single clay body is prepared, with different oxides added to each of three separate quantities of clay. The three colored clay slabs are being cut into collage strips. The tool is a linoleum knife with its point rounded and duller to prevent cutting the canvas-covered work surface.

Fig. 5-2　The contrasting clay slabs are cut into strips of various widths. The pupil will find this variety interesting in constructing a collage. Note the plasticity of the clay strips at this stage.

Fig. 5-3 In this collage construction the strips of clay are placed next to, or over, each succeeding application in an alternating manner. This is the bottom, or back side, of the collage. To prevent the finished work from cracking or pulling apart, the fingers are used to press and slide one clay strip firmly into the adjoining strip.

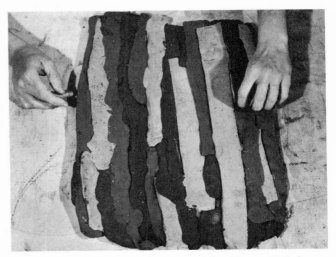

Fig. 5-4 The finished work is now right side up. Note how the canvas work surface serves to flatten the individual segments into a unit. The collage may best be turned over before firing by placing another rigid surface on top of the work and then switching the position. A firm work surface for transporting and drying of a clay collage is essential.

Fig. 5-5 It is characteristic of most collage shapes that are prepared from the reverse side to show the canvas texture. Note how strongly this texture is imprinted into the clay surface. A uniform texture tends to unify extremely complex works such as this one, which contains many individual segments.

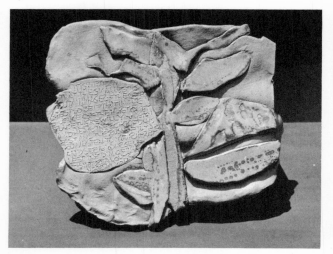

Figs. 5-6—5-7 A somewhat different collage approach is used in this work. A recognizable subject emerges, a legend is inscribed, and partial glazing is used to add variety. A needle or long pin attached to a wooden handle works well as a lettering tool for the development of such an inscription in clay.

This is the back treatment of the same work, in which a variety of flat shapes, rather than strips, is utilized. The interlocking of these shapes is attained by sliding the clay over and into the adjoining shape.

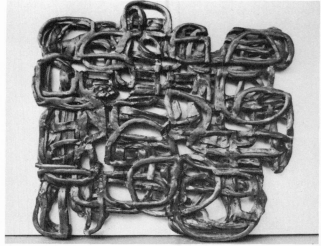

Fig. 5-8 An abstract expressionist style is shown in this clay collage. A white glaze was brushed over the heavily textured work. Glaze may often help tie together individual components of a collage.

Fig. 5-9 Extremely thin strips of clay are intertwined and overlapped in this lacy collage. A complex work like this is difficult to hold together, since the stress between its individual segments is particularly strong. A glaze covers most of this collage design.

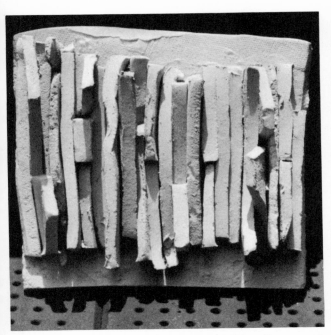

Fig. 5-10 In the previous collage examples, all segments were applied to overlap each succeeding part. In this unique work the strips of clay are laid on edge, pressed together near the base slab. Note the variety of heights and lengths of clay used in this work, producing darks and lights.

Fig. 5-11 Collage strips cast deep shadows when a variety of heights is used. Vertically applied lengths of clay often give a mosaic quality to the work.

The center cavity of this solid shape
was formed on a modeling wheel.

6. Solid-Formed Shapes

Perhaps in no other method of forming clay is the composition of the clay body so important as it is in the development of sculptured solid-formed shapes. It can be discouraging to work diligently on a sculptural form and find that unequal stress during the firing procedure, or a gas pocket or too-rapid drying has caused cracking or breaking of the piece.

First, determine a clay body that is proved to have a particularly low shrinkage factor. It is useful to try a simple shrinkage test, as shown in Fig. 6-1 before a group exploration is attempted. Select several combinations of clay with varying amounts of grog or body texture. A slab size is determined, 6″ x 6″ x ½″ thick. By using this measure, slabs of the various clays to be tested are allowed to dry thoroughly, and then fired in the kiln to Cone 1. (See Chapter 11 for a full description of firing procedures.) After firing, place each tile within a pencil-drawn 6″ square, as illustrated. It can be seen readily which clays will offer the most sculptural porosity and the least shrinkage. In most cases, grog (in ample quantity) is a primary safety factor in clays to be used in a sculptural or solid-formed process, since nongrogged clay bodies often shrink 10 to 20 per cent more than do heavily grogged clays.

Still another important consideration when bisqueing, or first firing, in the solid-formed process is to dry the piece very slowly and thoroughly. After this air-drying has been completed, it is helpful to store the solid-clay shape near the warm kiln, allowing the escaping warmth from the kiln to mature the clay further and reduce the effects of shock and stress that will come later, during the actual kiln firing. This undue stress can be clearly demonstrated by preparing a small, solid-clay block, even air-drying it, and then placing the block in a campfire or fireplace. It is important to be shielded from flying fragments of clay, as in just a few moments the sudden heat stress tends to disintegrate the clay.

A watertight glaze may be applied in the interior opening of the solid form before the initial firing. This is not usually recommended unless a minimum of glazing is done on a work, or, frequently, as a time-saver, the initial (bisque) firing in the solid-formed process is also the final firing, which may go as high as Cone 6 in most electric kilns. Many sculptural clays, however, will achieve quite satisfactory surface quality at Cone 1.

The solid-formed process lends itself to most forms of surface decoration, particularly stamping or pressing into the clay surface, since the solid mass can withstand such pressure without danger of misshaping or distorting the original shape too much.

If a disadvantage exists in a group situation in this forming process, it could be in the greater use and expenditure of the raw materials. This may or may not be critical, but needs to be considered, especially with large-group experimentation. However, the process can be adequately experienced by students by placing a limitation on the size of the actual forms to be developed. For instance, a solid form can be constructed (with an interior cavity) to be no larger than 3″ tall and 2″ wide, as is shown in Fig. 6-5. The interior cavity was formed by turning and pressing a ¾″ wooden dowel into the clay block. Clay corks were fashioned to fit as stoppers in the cavity. An additional suggestion on forming the interior core or cylindrical opening in a solid form is to vary or widen the opening at the top. To

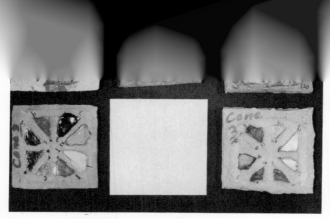

Fig. 6-1 Five different clay bodies were tested by shaping 6″-square slabs; each slab was ½″ thick. The white shape indicates the original size of each tile. The slab tile directly above the white shape is ungrogged, which accounts for the greater percentage of shrinkage.

Fig. 6-2 To begin the solid-formed process, the desired amount of clay is shaped by being pounded into the work surface and rotated so that it takes on a block or rectangular appearance.

Fig. 6-3 A 1″ dowel is gently forced into the clay block. By turning and pressing, an opening, or well, is formed. For larger blocks, it is helpful to dig out a starter hole for the dowel.

Fig. 6-4 After the cavity has been formed in the solid block of clay, a wire may be used to reshape the outside. The skiving away of the surface often exposes the grog and adds surface variety.

do this, the dowel or another round shape can be worked into the solid form at an angle, rotating slowly until the opening is widened to the desired size and shape. For larger work it is best to dig out a smaller starting cavity before shaping with a dowel. If more pressure is applied during any phase of the rotation, an oval or semiround opening can be formed.

Experimentation with these and other approaches in the solid-formed process may produce a variety of fascinating and unique results.

Glossary terms: Porosity, watertight, solid-form.

SUGGESTED TOOLS AND MATERIALS FOR THE SOLID-FORMED PROCESS

Clay (heavily grogged)
Canvas (covered work surface)
Dowels (wooden, various sizes, 12″ long)
Cutoff wire
Modeling tools (for surface decoration)
Glaze (optional)

Fig. 6-5 A solid-formed shape need not require a great deal of clay—these small shapes are less than 3″ tall. Solid shapes take surface designing well: note the repeat pattern developed by using the head of a nail set, or driving punch. The corks are shaped to the proper size by pressing and turning into the opening when the clay is leather-hard.

Fig. 6-6 The sides of the solid form need not be cut if it is desired that the outside shape retain its rounded, kneaded appearance. Note that the natural cleavage developed by handling is left as part of the character of the work.

The underside of Fig. 7-14 reveals
both the pounding or paddling of the
clay over the interior form and the
glaze application.

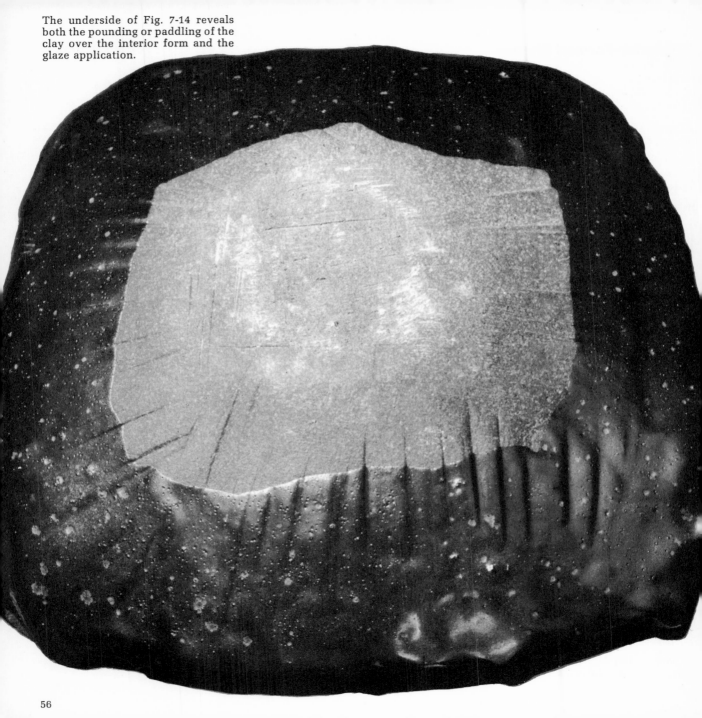

7. Interior-Formed Shapes

Almost any shape that is free of undercuts or overhangs may be used as an interior form. Round rocks, plaster forms and utilitarian shapes traditionally have been used for this purpose.

There is, however, a much more individualized method, and that is to design and build the form with clay. When the clay shape has dried, it reacts to moisture in much the same way as a plaster form would. Dry clay will absorb moisture and tend to dehydrate any applied slab of clay quite quickly.

For the purpose of demonstration, a form is developed by mounding a lump of clay on the canvas work panel (Fig. 7-1). Note that the sides are sloped and that there are no undercuts (Fig. 7-2), since these would tend to trap the applied clay and prevent a release from the form. By providing a slight tapering of the shape, one can eliminate this kind of problem. As shown in Fig. 7-3 the top of the dried-clay interior form has a carved handle to facilitate its removal from the work. If the drying period of the applied slab is gauged carefully, the interior form may be pulled free without undue pressure, thus eliminating damage to either the work or the form.

The clay paddles shown in Fig. 7-16 are simple handmade forming tools that can be used to flatten the slab gently and shape it over the clay form. The outer top ridge, or lip, of the finished slab plate frequently shows the potter's finger marks, which are left as part of the character of the finished piece.

As a variation, a carved design could be fashioned in the surface of the clay form so that the plate or bowl may have a relief design appearing in its interior face.

There are many other devices that can be employed in the interior-formed process. By fashioning a thin plastic sleeve over a section of cardboard tubing or a smooth-sided can, a pupil may then wrap a clay slab over the form and pull away a cylindrical form. By capping the end of such cylinders, the pupil may build a variety of containers or bottle shapes. The original clay form allows students to develop designs uniquely their own.

The example in Fig. 7-15 shows the bottom detail of a finished work that is left unglazed except for a small amount of excess glaze that spilled over from the inside surface. This dry-footing, or limited glazing, of the work makes stacking of the kiln a more simple matter. A byproduct of dry-footing is the change in design of the piece itself by allowing a contrast between the glaze and the exterior's textured natural-clay surface.

While the clay interior form will absorb quite rapidly the necessary moisture from a draped clay slab, there is a stage in its drying when the slab shape should be removed from the form. The student should attempt to lift off the applied shape as soon as it is rigid or strong enough to stand without slumping or becoming misshapen (Fig. 7-8). Allowing the clay slab to remain too long over the form will cause it to shrink tightly, become trapped and crack. Force-drying is another innovation to hasten maturing of the applied clay. The use of an electric fan (Fig. 7-7) increases air movement over the work and permits earlier removal of the slab from the form.

There is a distinct advantage in making the original model or form from clay. The cleanup is considerably easier when compared to similar plaster forms. The clay forms may also be reclaimed and reused as workable clay when a project is completed. In addition, the hardened clay interior form may be carved or altered in shape and in surface design quite readily. This kind of adaptability is not as possible with many other forms that are made of durable or rigid materials.

The interior clay process is perhaps the simplest in the younger child's exploration in developing clay forms. Overcoming the factor of limiting undercuts from the original design shape would be the most serious problem for each pupil, but once he has solved it, he can go on to achieve highly individual success in this process.

Glossary terms: Interior form, undercuts, cylindrical form, slumping, force-drying.

SUGGESTED TOOLS AND MATERIALS FOR THE INTERIOR-FORMED PROCESS

Clay (heavily grogged)
Simple clay-carving tools
Canvas-covered work boards or surfaces
Wooden paddles
Glaze
Brushes for glaze

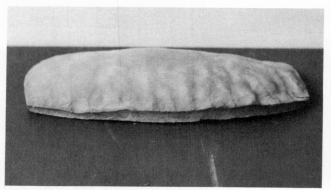

Fig. 7-1 A simple clay shape has been formed; its contour is rounded and free of undercuts. This shape will determine the interior cavity of the applied clay. It takes several days for a solid shape like this to dry enough for use as an interior form.

Fig. 7-2 By using a hacksaw blade, the completely dry shape may be scraped to remove small bumps and undercuts. This scraping helps to clean, or true, the form. Direct cutting and carving may be attempted if an interior raised design is desired in the slab trays that will be pulled from this shape.

Fig. 7-3 A clay interior form, because of its semifragile condition, is easier to handle if a hand grip is carved in its base. This grip need not be more than two parallel gouged-out areas with a space between for the handle.

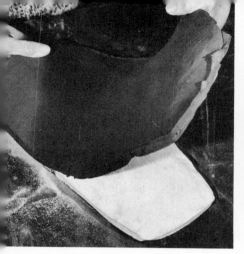

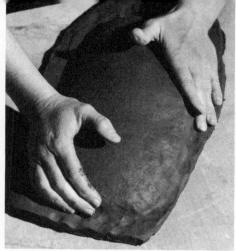

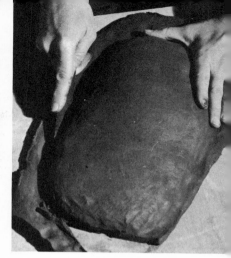

Fig. 7-4 After the solid shape has dried and the tooling has been completed, a fresh slab of clay is prepared. This slab is cut larger than the interior form. Overhangs will be removed after the slab is pressed into place.

Fig. 7-5 The applied slab of clay is molded to the interior shape by pressing the damp clay firmly around the model. Note the excess clay, which may be trimmed closely or allowed to remain extended as a lip on the tray.

Fig. 7-6 In the trimming process, the rounded edge of a hacksaw blade works well as a tool. (Sharp, pointed knives usually cut into the canvas-covered work surface.) The excess clay trimings may be used to fashion a foot to the tray if desired.

Fig. 7-7 To speed the drying of an applied clay shape, an electric fan is most helpful. A slowly rotating turntable, as shown here, will expose several such works to the fan's air circulation and will stiffen the pieces much more quickly than would otherwise be possible.

Fig. 7-8 After the clay has stiffened sufficiently to retain its shape, it is removed from the interior form. In most cases the top lip may still be manipulated and shaped with the fingers. If a foot is to be added to the piece, it should be attempted while the shape is still over the clay form.

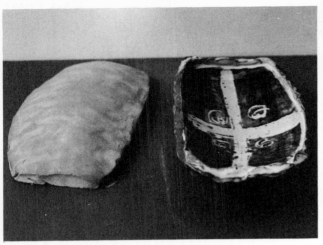

Fig. 7-9 Here are the finished tray and the original clay form. In this process the shrinkage factor is not very noticeable since the applied clay initially extended over and beyond the form, rather than being maintained inside it. Note the wax-resist brushed design, exposed through a darker top glaze.

Fig. 7-10 Many variations of glazing may be attempted when more than one of the same shape are reproduced. Note the variety created by the placement of the dark glaze strips.

Fig. 7-12 Repeat shapes often allow experimentation in glazes that may not be convenient or appropriate in one-of-a-kind works. This is a wet-in-wet application of several contrasting glazes.

Fig. 7-11 Designing with glaze offers a pupil additional challenges when a single clay shape is repeated. This is an example of a trailed-on glaze line design.

Fig. 7-13 This interior-formed work has not yet been fired. Note the inner-lip textural design and the stamped impressions in the interior surface.

Fig. 7-14 The hand of the artist shows clearly in this bowl shape. The finger-pressed edge of the lip is left to become an individualized part of the character of the work.

Fig. 7-16 Any flat-sided object may serve as a paddle to shape clay. Handles may be cut to make the tool easier to use. Note the heavy grain in the paddle at left; it tends to leave an added texture to the clay surface.

Fig. 7-15 This view of a ceramic tray reveals the bottom, which is left entirely unglazed. The glazing of shallow, non-footed trays and bowls on the exterior is often unnecessary since so little of that part of the work is exposed to view.

The lid of a container may be designed to comment the total work. This lid shape was form
pressing clay into a coffee-can lid.

8. Exterior-Formed Shapes

As with the other methods of forming objects from clay, there are several ways of exterior forming. Even pulp paper cartons can be used as exterior forms, as shown in two examples in Fig. 8-21. These examples of exterior-mold shapes were made by pressing damp clay into pulp-paper containers. The branch bottle on the left was formed separately in two berry containers and then joined. Two egg-carton tops were used to form the shape of the long, flat weed bottle. An added advantage of temporary molds such as these is that the shape of the mold often suggests further design, such as the form and placement of the opening or the glaze treatment utilizing inherent texture and lines in the crude mold.

Basically, any means of outside, or exterior, support that can temporarily hold a clay shape will do. For the illustration, traditional plaster is cast as the form device. One suggestion that needs to be considered when using plaster in a group exploration is to provide the necessary preparatory and clean-up arrangements prior to actual mixing and pouring. Often undue haste may develop as the plaster begins to harden or if sufficient plaster is not prepared ahead to accommodate the experience at hand.

An original model from clay, solid and without undercuts, is made directly on the canvas-covered work board, which is covered with wax paper. This is done for two reasons: (1) to protect the canvas work board from the adhering plaster, and (2) to allow a means of releasing the finished cast. As shown in the photograph in Fig. 8-1, the basic idea for a bowl shape is developed by working directly in the clay upside down, or with concern only for the basic outside shape and not with the inner, or hollow, cavity. After the bowl shape has been completed, with slightly beveled sides to allow for easy removal, a bottomless box shape is placed around the model (Fig. 8-2). Heavy cardboard, thin sheet metal or wood serve equally well as form-construction materials. To maintain a somewhat uniform mold shape, supporting clay lumps are pressed against the cardboard to avoid stress points. Masking tape is also used to reinforce corners and to make the plaster wall reasonably leakproof.

The plaster-pouring process is easy if certain steps are taken. It is preferable to make this mold pouring in one operation; thus, sufficient plaster must be prepared in advance. Plaster of paris or casting plaster may be mixed in several ways. For the exterior-mold process the mixing container must be large enough to prepare more than enough plaster to cover the entire clay model. The plaster-mixing process involves filling the container with water to approximately three fourths of its total volume. Dispersing of the plaster by hand is done in a rotating fashion into the water, much like sowing seeds. This is done until a heavy, wet crust of bubbles begins to appear on the water's surface. After a few minutes, the mixture can be reached into to dissolve any remaining small pockets of dry or unmixed plaster. Then the mixture is poured into the prepared form at a stage when the plaster liquid seems medium thick in consistency and thoroughly homogenized. After pouring the plaster to the top of the cardboard well (allowing at least an inch above the clay form), the plaster mold should remain to cure for 24 hours before using. Since precautions were taken earlier to eliminate undercuts in the clay model, its release, or pulling away, from the plaster cast may be accomplished without the use of parting agents, such as oil. However, as an added precaution the clay model can be brushed over with a bar-soap solution and allowed to dry before casting.

After the plaster mold has dried sufficiently to become reasonably absorbent, a clay slab is prepared, ½″ in thickness and at least 6″ larger overall than the plaster form's well or opening (Fig. 8-6). This clay slab is draped into the form and gently pressed to conform to the walls and bottom (Fig. 8-7). Undue pressure in any one place may make the walls too thin in these spots. After the clay has taken on the mold's shape, the excess overlap may be trimmed away at the outer edge (Fig. 8-8). The clay bowl shape will tend to pull itself away from the plaster forms in a short time, perhaps in an hour, to allow safe removal (Fig. 8-9).

Further tooling or trimming may be attempted after the shape has matured and stiffened (Figs. 8-10, 8-11). As a variation or further experience, two bowl shapes may be produced from this single plaster exterior form. It is suggested that the first

clay shape pulled be covered with thin plastic to retard its drying while the other half is being developed in the mold. This simple precaution will often prevent cracks or splits from developing because of a difference in moisture content of adjoining parts. The double-mold and several other variations of the exterior-formed process are shown in Figs. 8-12—8-19.

Glossary terms: Exterior form, temporary molds, plaster of paris, casting plaster, draped clay.

SUGGESTED MATERIALS AND TOOLS FOR THE EXTERIOR-FORMED PROCESS

Clay
Clay-modeling tools
Canvas-covered work panel
Wax paper
Casting plaster
Plaster mixing pans
Cardboard form materials
Masking tape

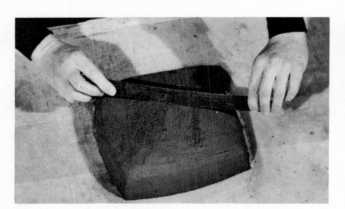

Fig. 8-1 A solid shape of clay is molded into a bowl form. To level the high and low areas, a hacksaw blade is scraped over the work. Note the sloping sides and the absence of undercuts.

Fig. 8-2 The model is framed with a cardboard fence, tied together at the joints with strips of masking tape. Lumps of damp clay are placed against the frame to avoid distortion of the mold. The walls of the frame are at least 1″ higher than the clay model.

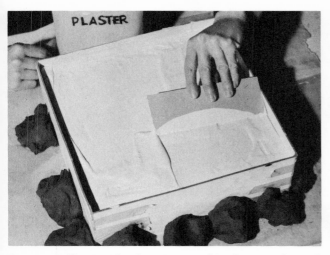

Fig. 8-3 Following the directions in this chapter, plaster is mixed and poured over the model. A mold of this size will begin to set in a short time. The cardboard frame can be pulled away as soon as the plaster has hardened.

Fig. 8-4 The exterior mold is now ready to use. The edges are trimmed, and the mold has had a 24-hour drying and curing period.

Fig. 8-5 The thickness of the mold is of some importance: the more plaster, the higher the water-absorption rate. This 3″-thick exterior form is sturdy and offers a quick means of reproducing a single shape.

Fig. 8-6 A slab of clay is draped into the form. At this stage the clay seems to mold better if it is about ½″ thick. Note that the slab is considerably larger than the mold opening.

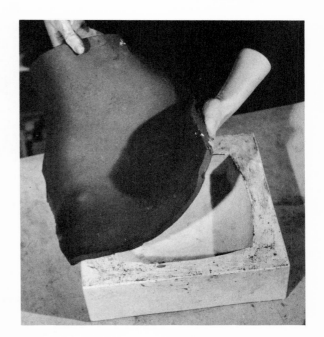

Fig. 8-7   After the clay slab is loosely draped into the form, gentle pressing allows the clay to conform to the mold's shape. Any thin spots may be patched at this time, using the same clay. Smoothing of the interior should also be attempted now.

Fig. 8-8   The excess clay is trimmed away with a straight knife or a thin hacksaw blade. The clay clings to the plaster-form walls quite tightly at this stage; however, as absorption begins, the separation of clay from plaster proceeds quickly.

Fig. 8-9   In an hour or less, the bowl shape has stiffened enough for safe removal from the mold. It is at this stage that final surface tooling or adding of clay is best attempted. The last finishing and sanding are done after waiting for the piece to reach a much drier state.

Fig. 8-10   Four small feet, fashioned from the same clay, are attached to the bowl shape. To fasten foot and body together the medium-soft clay is tooled with a modeling tool or a common pencil.

Fig. 8-11   A clay-ring footing is applied to the bowl. The ring is cut from a slab and curled around to form a circle, then placed on the bottom of the bowl, tooled into the body and hand-smoothed.

Fig. 8-12   In these examples of the finished shape, interior glazing is contrasted with exterior tooling. The footing serves to elevate the shape, eliminating a bottom-heavy appearance.

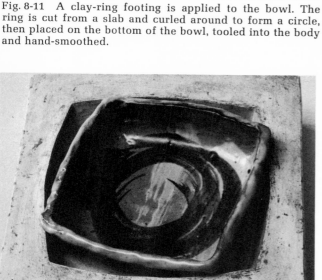

Fig. 8-13   The finished work graphically reveals the amount of shrinkage that takes place from the original mold size. Students often comment that their fired pieces seem much smaller than they remembered.

Fig. 8-14   These two individualized pieces have something in common: both are made by using the same exterior form. The bottle shape was constructed by joining two bowl shapes like the one at left. While the clay was damp, the closed shape had a neck attached. A slight joint, or ridge, still remains, but careful tooling and glazing modify the construction character of the work.

Fig. 8-15 The neck, or opening, treatment of these joined double-mold shapes is simple and direct. A single coil of clay is attached to the work and a hole is then cut through into the body.

Fig. 8-16 This open-finger or grid design is one variation of an exterior-formed piece. The original outline shape was cut from a ½"-thick slab of clay and allowed to form in a simple cheesecloth sling. During the drying process the cutaway ribs of the bowl were bent upward to form the bowl, or enclosed shape.

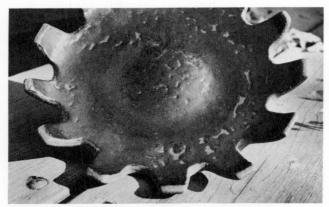

Fig. 8-17 A related cutout treatment is shown in this large platter, which was formed by shaping the clay slab into a large, round, canvas-lined metal tray. The black matte glaze was applied only to the interior face of the work, thus offering a contrast in surfaces.

Fig. 8-18 Wooden salad bowls were used to form this two-part, flat, round branch bottle. The finger marks left from squeezing the two bowl shapes together add an informal design facet to the work. A lightly brushed white glaze contrasts with the darker glaze poured over the spout.

Fig. 8-19 At first glance this container appears to have been constructed with many thin coils of clay. Actually, the ridges were formed by pressing a damp clay slab into double-sided corrugated paper. The clay was trimmed and then set upright and shaped into a cylindrical form. A heavy black matte glaze was applied, and no attempt was made to scrape the glaze away from the high ridges, as in other examples shown.

Fig. 8-20 This heavily ribbed container receives its texture from a corrugated cardboard exterior form. The glaze on the high ridges was scraped away before the glaze firing. Any textured flexible material that can be made into a tube may serve as an exterior-forming device.

Fig. 8-21 These unique exterior-formed shapes make use of very common forming devices. The square weed bottle on the left was formed from two paper berry boxes. The long, narrow container at right was made by pressing clay into the top lids of egg cartons. Note the interesting openings.

A variation of the envelope process shows how the larger side panels are bent or curved to fit a predetermined bottom and cap. Note the small openings, identifying the piece as a branch bottle.

9. Envelope-Formed Shapes

Perhaps no other slab-inspired hand-formed process in creating with clay is as informal and spontaneous, in a design sense, as is the envelope method; but perhaps none is also as unpredictable for the pupil. This becomes most apparent when a freshly formed slab of clay is cut and lifted from the clay board. The slab is sagging and pliable at this stage, and certainly not stable enough to hold as a free-standing shape.

It is obvious that some precautionary steps must be taken. A helpful procedure is to allow each slab of clay to mature and firm for several hours, or even overnight, to allow for some degree of control. If, after experimentation, it appears that the clay slab has become too firm and dry when left overnight, a loosely draped thin-plastic covering may be applied over the slab to slow down the drying and to keep the clay in workable condition.

The sequence in Figs. 9-1–9-4 illustrates how one might build an envelope container using slab walls. The clay is still somewhat pliable and can be squeezed without cracking. If the walls happen to be too stiff to zipper or to cross-tool the joints together with the fingers or a modeling tool, one can roughen the edges to be joined, then "butter" on slip and squeeze the joints closed. This is frequently the case with larger works, since slab parts of such pieces will have to span greater distances.

Envelope forms may or may not require side panels, or inserts, as shown in the demonstration. Curved and straight sides may be combined in some instances (Fig. 9-15). A unique variation is shown in the sculptural work in Fig. 9-17, where multiple envelope shapes have been combined and joined to form a single composition.

In the demonstration sequence, slabs about ⅜"

thick are being used to construct a flat bottle. This thickness is a minimum for many envelope shapes, but it is not necessary or even desirable if smaller sculptural pieces are to be formed as was the figure shown in Fig. 9-18, where several slabs of ¼" to ⅛" thickness were used in a related fold-over envelope technique. No predrying or maturing period need take place in this kind of procedure, as the clay is handled more easily while in a truly plastic condition. This has an advantage for sculptural shapes such as small animal forms or figures for which the clay used is soft enough to squeeze or press into the shapes desired.

By throwing the slabs as described on pages 72-73, one can quickly develop very thin-walled shapes, such as that shown in Fig. 9-18. Since most envelope forms have long seams or joints, it is often appropriate, in a design sense, to allow the seam pressings and joints to retain the mark of the hand or tool being used. As can be seen in the example in Figs. 9-11 and 9-12, the texture of the joined edges contributes to the overall surface design of the work. Note also the combination textural treatment using combined slip, glaze and sgraffito techniques in Fig. 9-10.

Whether the pupil attempts a sculptural figure or a vessel shape through the envelope process, the complete joining of slab shapes is important in order to avoid gaps or openings in the final fired form. This is particularly true of utility containers such as the Japanese-inspired hip container in Figs. 9-13 and 9-14, which is designed to carry water. Utilitarian vessels such as these should have the interior well thoroughly glazed to make them watertight.

It is best to try to complete an envelope form in

one session. If this is not possible the unfinished form, as well as the individual parts to be attached later, should be covered with thin plastic to retain the clay's workability.

Due to the quick method of joining edges, the envelope process has an advantage in permitting the older pupil to construct rather large works in a relatively short period. The younger child may develop small, delicate sculptural figures using a thinner slab.

The envelope method is perhaps best suited for those pupils who work best in a direct and spontaneous manner. It is a versatile process, allowing a wide range between utilitarian and sculptural works.

Glossary terms: Envelope form, sagging, cross-tooling, hip container.

SUGGESTED MATERIALS AND TOOLS FOR THE ENVELOPE-FORMED PROCESS

Canvas-covered clay boards (several)
Clay (grogged)
Knife (dull or rounded point)
Slip (for joining slabs)
Plastic (thin, garment covers)
Modeling tool (wooden, double-ended)

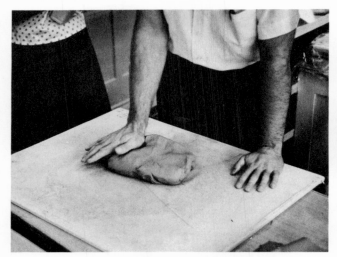

Fig. 9-1 In most methods of forming a slab of clay, the quantity of clay desired is first pressed into a thick, uneven, flat shape by hand. The palms of the hands serve well as the flattening tool. Slabs may be formed by pressing, pounding and, most commonly, by rolling—but throwing a slab is a unique method, and perhaps the quickest.

Fig. 9-2 The hand-flattened slab is picked up and held away from the body. Note that the clay, approximately 1″ thick at this stage, has already acquired the texture of the canvas-covered work surface.

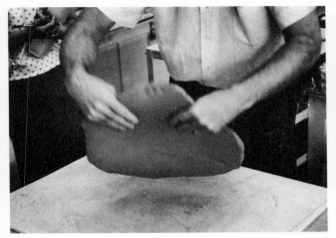

Fig. 9-3 The clay is being flipped, or thrown down and toward the body. It strikes the canvas surface in a sliding motion, causing a spreading and thinning of the clay mass. After a few practice throws, the procedure develops naturally.

Fig. 9-4 A uniformly thick ⅜″ slab of clay 18″ in diameter is produced by three throws. The time and effort involved are considerably less with the slab-throwing process than with the traditional rolling method.

Fig. 9-5 One remarkable feature of this quick, easy slab-forming is the resultant uniformity of thickness. Note that only at the extremities of the slab is there a thinning of the clay. Because the clay particles become more compressed and aligned than is usual in other methods, formation of slabs by throwing seems to give the clay an added measure of strength.

Fig. 9-6   After the plan for an envelope shape has been determined a slab is prepared, and the parts are cut and scored. Note the side-insert panels and the top, made ready to include in the construction process as it develops.

Fig. 9-7   With the clay in a pliable condition, the sides of the envelope are brought up and joined to the insert panels. The clay must be soft enough at this stage to allow squeezing the joints or edges together, yet still stiff enough to stand.

Fig. 9-8   When the shape has been closed on all sides the precut top and neck section is attached. The neck opening in this work was formed by folding clay around a pencil.

Fig. 9-9   After the final shaping and squeezing together of all parts of the envelope shape, the surface designing may be attempted.

Fig. 9-10 There are no side inserts in this envelope vase shape. The bottom slab is pushed upward and into the sides. Note the combination of wide brush strokes of several glazes, running in opposition to the sgraffito lines.

Fig. 9-11 This large envelope container stands over 24″ high. The side inserts extend above the front and back panels. The work is glazed overall, and an incised legend has been lettered with a pin scriber.

Fig. 9-12 The same vessel, viewed from another angle, reveals the side-insert construction. To glaze a large work like this, the piece is placed in a container on sticks and the glaze is poured over the work.

The inspiration for this envelope may have been the traditional Japanese ceramic hip flash. The glazing of the side paneling indicates the use of several methods: brushing, pouring and slip trailing.

Fig. 9-14 Another view of the same hip flash shows the spout ring, a coil of clay added to the top cap of the piece over a precut opening.

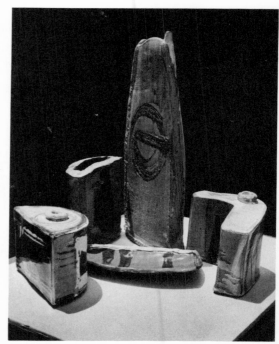

Fig. 9-15 This envelope shape is designed to contrast curved and straight sides. The light-colored underglaze was brushed over with a wax-resist design, then covered with a deep-brown glaze that, when fired, allowed the waxed design to appear.

Fig. 9-16 Several envelope shapes are juxtaposed here with an interior-formed platter shape. Note the bold use of the large-brush, single-stroke glaze application.

Fig. 9-17 Envelope construction lends itself to sculptural techniques, as is seen in this multiform shape. The appendages are hollow. Note that the joined edges have been paddled to give them a heavy, strong appearance. A rod extending from the wooden base into the work supports the piece.

Fig. 9-18 This thin slab figure was constructed by the fold-over technique; the clay was squeezed and modeled while in a wet, pliable condition.

A very informal approach to constructing containers is seen in these two envelope vessels. One long strip of clay is joined in the center, with the bottom folded up over the sides.

10. Surface Design and Decoration

Perhaps no other area of clay experimentation offers the student an opportunity to stretch his imagination as much as does surface designing and decorating. He has an endless choice of tools, none of which need be sophisticated or expensive.

Interesting designs and patterns can be developed by utilizing common kitchen utensils and other ordinary objects. For instance, corrugated paper can be used effectively to produce a ribbed surface; a spool can be used to produce an overall dotted pattern; a carved cork can be used in developing a pressed-relief design. All of these methods that use inexpensive tools combine to excite and encourage the student to expand upon ways of enhancing the clay's surface.

There are two choices in changing a clay's surface: to *add* to the original surface, or to *subtract* from it. The wide range of possibilities in mixing these two alternatives brings suspense and excitement to the student.

Surface Addition: Glaze, the most common additive as a ceramic decorative medium, may be poured into or over a work, or the piece may be immersed or dipped into glaze, or the glaze may be trailed onto a surface. Spraying of glaze, not recommended for students because of its toxicity factor, is best suited to industrial and commercial applications. It is in the brush application of glaze that students most often have successful experiences with glazing.

Developing a Glaze Formula: Many technical books on ceramics offer valuable, though often complicated, suggestions for specific formulas for glaze development. However, it is recommended that pupils who prefer to explore their own glaze formulation, rather than use prepared glazes, start with a very simple glaze-formula base. A particularly simple base glaze is described here that utilizes only two primary ingredients—colemanite and red clay in equal proportions.

The Base Glaze

Colemanite	50%
Red clay	50%

If the red clay being used is lumpy and hard, it should be crushed first to a reasonably small aggregate or powder and placed in a mixing jar with an equal amount of powdered colemanite. Then, by adding enough water to make a heavy, creamy brushing consistency, the base glaze is ready for use. This base glaze produces a rich, high-luster, semitransparent brown color. The brown color varies; it is derived from an inherent quantity of the iron oxide found in red clay.

Colemanite facilitates and promotes the melting and fusing of the base mix at a practical or reasonably low temperature. A Cone 1, or 2,153°F, firing produces excellent results with this initial formula. Colemanite base glaze may also be formulated by substituting another clay called P.V. (plastic vitrox) in the same proportions. A simple two-part glaze can become a three-part glaze by adding oxides. The glaze color may be changed to the following:

Color	Additive	Percentage of the Total
Orange-brown	Red iron oxide	10%
Blue	Cobalt oxide	2%
Yellow	Tin vanadium stain	10%

By adding 10% zircopax or any other glaze opacifier to the original glaze ingredients, the basic glaze formula may be changed further to produce an opaque or milky characteristic. This kind of experimentation in glaze formulation is not too complex for students, yet will add a new facet to their experience in ceramics.

The following suggestions for glaze selection and application are offered to help students achieve reasonably satisfactory results.

Glazing Characteristics to Consider:
- Glaze should enhance the original form and not obscure or diminish its impact.
- The brushing consistency of glaze should approach that of heavy cream.
- Naturally hard-to-see areas of a work, such as the insides of containers or vessels, are often enhanced by lighter glaze colors.
- Running of glaze is usually caused by overfiring the glaze beyond the recommended cone temperature for the glaze ingredients or formulation.
- Dry-footing, or nonglazing, of the bottom of objects is highly recommended to diminish kiln-stacking problems, grinder work or sanding, and in general as a safety consideration.
- A wax-resist application assists in dry-footing and is an excellent method of determining glaze boundaries.
- An opaque glaze minimizes the translucent quality of the glazed surface except on protruding areas and ridges, where glaze becomes thinner and exposes more of the body color.

Several Methods of Applying Glaze:
- Brush application is the most economical way to experiment with glaze; less is wasted than with other methods.
- The dipping method of glazing is the quickest, though not always the most suitable, since a large quantity of glaze is needed.
- The spray process of applying glaze is perhaps

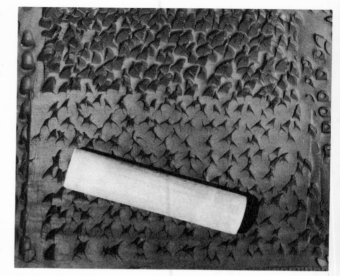

Fig. 10-1   Initial surface designing in clay may be subdued or altered by paddling, or by rolling lightly over the original impressions, as shown.

Fig. 10-2   An unlimited variety of clay-texturing tools may be employed. The utility items used offer a contrast with the finger impressions on the far left.

the most wasteful and the most toxic. The final result is sometimes impressive, but should be attempted only in highly controlled situations.

- The glaze-pouring method, originally intended for glazing large works too big for dipping, is an effective means for partial glazing and spectacular runoffs, or spreading.
- The trailing of glaze is a highly individualized method, relying on lines of glaze to project a design or surface pattern.
- The flipping of glaze with a brush causes a random splatter effect, which is often quite dramatic. Glaze is usually flipped over a base or underglaze.
- The pressing or blotting of glaze, using a flat surface, or knotted-yarn or string method utilizes the soaking of a shape or highly absorbent string with glaze and wrapping or pressing the wet glazed item over an underglazed surface. The random blots of glaze add an irregular textural facet to the glaze application.

The photographs on the following pages show variations of these basic methods of surface texturing and glaze application.

Glossary terms: Dipping, trailing, toxicity factor, colemanite, iron oxide, zircopax, opaque, translucent.

Fig. 10-3 Repeat-texturing devices may be fashioned from clay, then fired. This group consists of a single stamp at right, a double-figure repeat in the center and a dot-dash roller on the left.

Fig. 10-4 A texture roller gives the sides of this bowl a relief design. The clay is at medium-firm consistency to prevent collapse or distortion of the work.

Fig. 10-5 The sides of this vessel have been decorated with a single stamp. A sandpaper block is used to dimish portions of the impressed designs.

Fig. 10-6 A combination of surface scratching and clear glazing give this multiform shape a rough surface.

Fig. 10-7 Note the directional changes in the texture pattern of this detailed view of the previous work. Glazing and texturing were produced simultaneously.

Fig. 10-8 A unique method of glaze application in this work produced a repeat pattern of glaze alternating with bare clay. This was accomplished by channeling grooves in the damp clay, applying glaze overall and then scraping the glaze away from the high levels.

Fig. 10-9 Test glaze-formula samplers are easily mixed in temporary containers. By adding water, dry-glaze ingredients may be made readily usable.

Fig. 10-10 This tile glaze sampler is decorated with a stencil technique of glaze application. Glaze is applied through a perforated screen over an underglazed background.

Fig. 10-11 An overall pattern using finger impressions makes a striking surface design. Note that the glaze application slumps to the lower impressions after firing; the high ridges show the clay-body color.

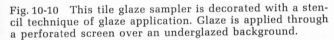

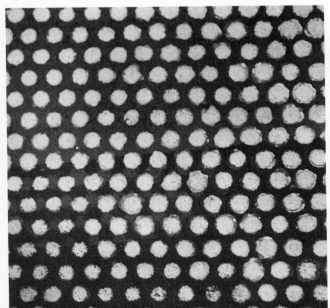

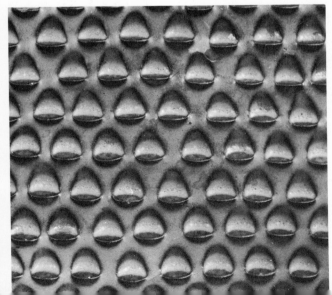

Fig. 10-13 This informal watery glaze pattern was accomplished with a wet-in-wet application. The thin top glaze is applied with a brush; then the bowl is tipped to allow the glaze to run down the sides.

Fig. 10-14 A repeat spool pattern appears in this glazed tile. Note that the glaze thins, or burns away, at the edges of the designed areas.

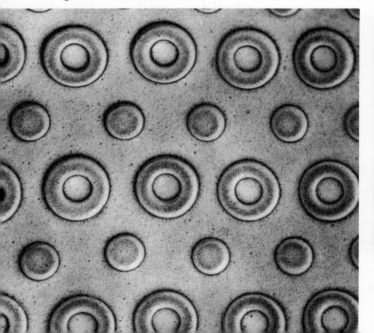

Fig. 10-15 The heavy iron-glaze application on this bowl partially obscures the surface carving. The gouged texture was created with the round end of a paper clip.

Fig. 10-16 This hanging vessel was formed with stoneware, or high-fired clay. The glaze treatment includes an initial overall application of white. Masking tape is next applied in a resist design over the white glaze and then covered with an iron-black glaze. The final firing exposes the masked area.

Fig. 10-17 White slip is poured unevenly over the scratched surface of this container, then covered with a random application of ash glaze to produce a combination of surface textures. Several distinct textures were created by using more than one technique.

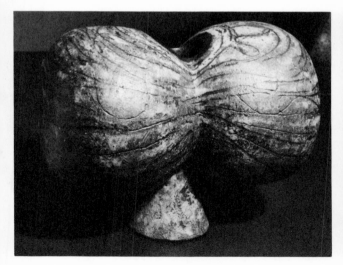

Fig. 10-18 This multiform shape utilizes a single glaze—a white matte formulation. The line design on the container's surface is scratched through the glaze into the clay (a sgraffito technique).

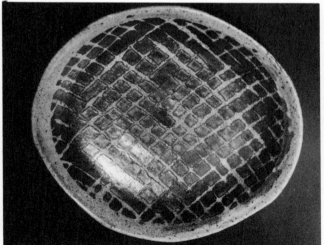

Fig. 10-19 The striking net pattern of this slab plate derives from the use of a small brush and wax emulsion. Then iron slip is brushed over the entire waxed design before bisque firing. To finish the work a clear glaze is used to cover the bisqued design in the last firing.

Fig. 10-20 The glaze technique used on this long-necked bottle combines several methods. A wax-resist medium is trailed over a portion of the white underbody glaze. Then a sharp instrument is used to scratch away some of the wax so that both white and black lines emerge after final firing.

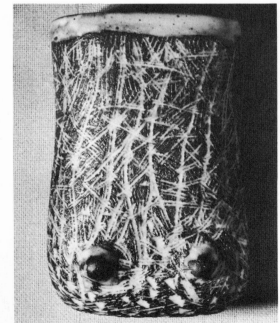

Fig. 10-21 An iron stain is poured over a matte underglaze surface on this stoneware vase. Note the interesting uneven runoffs of stain. The lip of the vessel is left unglazed.

Fig. 10-22 This hanging vessel shows the use of the sponge-off technique. First, the surface design is scratched on. Following the bisque firing, the object is dipped in white glaze. After the glaze has dried, a sponge is used to wipe off most of the surface glaze, allowing the etched lines to remain white against the unglazed body color.

The dry-footing of these items is extreme; however, it offers a great contrast between the glaze and clay body.

These two bowls show different approaches to footing. The pieces are totally glazed except for the last ⅜″ of the footings.

11. Firing Procedures

The chief organic characteristic of fired clay is a stonelike hardness. To change raw clay to this durable state requires exposure to prolonged and intense fire. The four major sources of kiln heat are electricity, gas, oil and wood. Many older cultures, such as Japan, still rely primarily on a wood fire as the source of heat to fire their ceramics. Gas kilns are becoming more common in the classroom, where they are used extensively to produce extremely high-fire reduction stoneware. For most studio and classroom needs, electric kilns are perhaps the most practical in providing clay experiences for the student. These electric kilns are compact, need less in the way of special facilities and are economical to operate. Many electric kiln manufacturers offer, as standard equipment, automatic cutoffs, which are safety devices vital in providing maximum safety of the kiln and of the materials being fired. In structural design, electric kilns are available as either front- or top-loaders.

Preparing the Kiln for Firing: It is important to prepare the kiln shelves by applying a coating of kiln wash to the top of each shelf. This wash will prevent glaze drops and ceramic pieces from adhering to the shelves during firing. The kiln wash should be applied only to the tops of the shelves and to the bottom bricks of the kiln. Since kiln wash contains pure silica, it should not come in contact with the walls of the kiln or be splashed on the wiring elements, as the silica content will cause the wires to melt and burn through.

Loading the Kiln: Pyrometric cones are commercially available in two common sizes: small and large (junior and senior). Before selecting cones, one must determine the best method to be used in controlling the temperature of a particular kiln. For instance, if the kiln has an automatic cutoff mechanism, the junior cone would be normally used. If, however, the kiln-cutoff control is to be manipulated visually and manually, then the larger (senior) cone would be utilized. In both cases cones rely on the same principle. Each cone number (.06, .05, .04, and so on) determines the melting or bending point of the cone's composition, that is, the mixture of ingredients that make up the cone itself. Pyrometric-cone manufacturers use quality-control testing methods to ensure a standard and reasonably accurate prediction device of the kiln's interior heat. Although some kilns do come equipped with a temperature gauge, a pyrometer that reveals the degree of a kiln's interior heat by visual observation (some actually cut off the power at a designated temperature), most potters continue to rely on the cone as their best barometer. For the classroom and most studio kiln installations, the automatic cutoff devices, which are underwriter approved, offer convenience and a margin of safety that are well worth considering.

If the kiln has an automatic cutoff control, the setting of this device must be accomplished before loading the kiln. If the kiln does not have such a device, a provision should be made to include a cone-setting arrangement on one of the kiln shelves in such a position that allows viewing through one of the kiln's peepholes. Since hot spots may develop in many kilns because of uneven loading, it is recommended that the cones be placed at least 1" away from large pieces or the kiln's heating elements.

The Bisque, or Initial, Fire: The first firing of a clay object is its most critical hurdle to maturity. If the work survives the initial bake, then the success of succeeding glaze firings without structural mishap seems assured.

All clay items should be thoroughly dry before being loaded into the kiln. The clay should have a soft, dry feel as opposed to a cool dampness. The care taken in stacking the kiln for a bisque fire is not quite so critical a factor as it is with a glaze firing. However, the work is fragile at this stage and cannot be expected to stand heavy stacking or positioning that encourages breakage or warping. It is recommended that the bisque fire be set low, at Cone .09. This does not mean that the higher-temperature cones will not produce a satisfactory bisque. A rule of thumb is that glaze applications are achieved more easily when the bisque is soft and porous, and not fired too high. The lower the bisque fire, the easier it is to apply glaze to the ceramic body.

To avoid stress and shock to items being fired, it is often a good practice to allow a prefiring of items in the kiln. (Low heat only, with the door propped open wide for several hours.) Next, to schedule the firing of bisqueware properly, this sequence should be followed:

1. Set cone, prop kiln lid open with firebrick or kiln post (approximately 2″), and leave *low heat* on for one hour.
2. Next, turn *medium heat* on for an additional hour, leaving kiln lid in propped position as before.
3. Check kiln atmosphere. If heat escaping from kiln is dry, remove prop and carefully close lid. At this stage, turn *high heat* on.
4. Leave top peephole unplugged during full firing schedule to allow release of remaining gas vapors and moisture.
5. After the cone bends (determined either visually or by automatic cutoff mechanism), allow kiln to cool sufficiently to ensure safe removal and handling of all pieces fired.

The Glaze Fire: After bisque firing, the individual pieces are readied for glazing. Before applying glaze, remove or blow away loose particles of clay and clay dust, as these will alter the final surface quality if left on.

After the liquid glaze has been applied and allowed to become totally dry, the cold kiln may be loaded. Care should be taken to see that each item loaded into the kiln has sufficient clearance, both from adjacent works and from the interior kiln walls and heating elements. Dry-footing of the work being fired makes this part of the kiln-stacking operation smoother, requiring less handling and time. The general rule is that a glaze firing must be at a higher temperature than the original (bisque) firing. The clay bisque and the glaze should reach the fusing temperature simultaneously. It is not always possible to ensure a satisfying glazed surface automatically, however, since glaze maturation or fluxing temperatures vary with each glaze formula. As an example, certain intense bright colors that normally fuse at Cone .05 will disappear almost entirely if fired to Cone 1. Matte glazes usually will not fuse properly unless fired at higher temperatures than most high-gloss glazes.

The suggested five-step firing sequence for bisqueware may be also followed for glaze firing, with modifications in the early steps, which may be shortened since the work has proven to be stable through the bisque firing. Cone requirements of the glazes used will need to be different, that is, at a higher temperature than was used for the bisque firing. A guide to pyrometric cones and temperature equivalents, along with suggested kiln characteristics and related process considerations, are provided on pages 91-93.

Glossary terms: Kiln wash, junior cone, senior cone, kiln elements.

The Anatomy of a Kiln

A. *Kiln lid* (constructed of insulating firebrick)
B. *Heating elements* (imbedded in grooves of insulating brick)
C. *Switch box* (one for each kiln ring)
D. *Power cutoff* (uses small cone to shut down kiln automatically)
E. *Pilot light* (light is on when elements are heating)
F. *Power cord* (heavy-duty 4-blade plug assembly)
G. *Air space* (allows heat to dissipate)
H. *Leg supports* (used to elevate kiln from floor)
I. *Kiln jacket* (holds firebrick in place)
J. *Upper peephole* (never closed; used for interior observation)
K. *Kiln-lid brace* (holds kiln door open during early stages of firing)

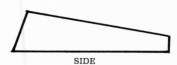

END   SIDE

TEMPERATURES AND CONES
(fahrenheit)

KILN TEMPERATURE

KILN TEMPERATURE	PYROMETRIC CONES NO.
2471° F.	12
2437	11
2426	10
2403	9
2372	8
2307	7
2291	6
2230	5
2208	4
2185	3
2154	2
2153	1
2152	01
2098	02
2068	03
2008	04
1944	05
1873	06
1846	07
1801	08
1751	09
1686	010
1680	011
1650	012
1615	013
1596	014
1549	015

These temperature equivalents refer specifically to the *small cones* used extensively in kiln-safety mechanisms such as automatic cutoffs. The cone information adapted here was obtained from the Edward Orton Jr. Ceramic Foundation, Columbus, Ohio.

During steps 1 and 2 of the firing process, the kiln door is allowed to remain open at least 2".

THE PROCESS		KILN CHAMBER COLOR
PORCELAIN FIRE	CONE 12	WHITE
HIGH FIRE CHINA & STONEWARE GLAZE FIRE	CONE 8 TO 10	LIGHT YELLOW
ELECTRIC KILN STONEWARE GLAZE FIRE (FELDSPOTHIC)	CONE 4 TO 8	YELLOW
EARTHENWARE GLAZE FIRE (LEADED & STRONG FLUX GLAZES)	CONE .04 TO 4	YELLOW-ORANGE
LOWFIRE CLAY GLAZE FIRE (BRIGHT REDS AND ORANGES)	CONE .06	ORANGE
CLAY BISQUE FIRE (FIRST FIRE)	CONE .09 TO .04	RED-ORANGE
ENAMELING AND GLASS FORMING FIRE	CONE .015	RED
FIRING TIME	A TIME LAPSE OF APPROXIMATELY TEN HOURS FROM COLD KILN TO CONE 6. AN ADDITIONAL TWO HOURS TO CONE 12.	

A suggested kiln-firing guide for classroom or studio.

12. Organization for Clay Experiences

Certain steps should be taken to ensure the best possible management and working conditions for experimenting with clay.

Perhaps the prime consideration should be the plan used in the dispensing and storage of the materials, primarily the clays and glazes. For our purposes these fall into five distinct categories or needs: (1) dispensing of clay, (2) salvage of materials, (3) care of materials, (4) handling of tools and equipment, and (5) display and mounting of the clay product.

Prepackaged clay used in studio work or in classroom exploration undergoes a four-step procedure before it is ready to be used.

1. First, the raw, or unprocessed, clay is converted into a liquid form (slip). This is done in a mixing tank called a blunger. Impurities such as rocks, sticks and other foreign matter are removed by a screening procedure at this time.

2. Next, the liquid clay is combined with additional matter such as grog, oxides or other clay bodies, and is put into a filter press. Air pressure is used to force the clay into the press, forming semidry round cakes of clay as shown in Fig. 12-1.

3. The third step involves inserting the round cakes of clay into a pug mill, as shown in Fig. 12-2. The function of the pug mill is to blend the clay ingredients thoroughly. Since ·the cakes of clay are not heretofore mixed evenly, the pug mill works the raw mixture until the clay is homogenized and uniform in consistency.

4. The last steps are the extruding of clay from the pug mill, shown in Fig. 12-3, and finally the packaging.

Since professional clay processors make many clay formulas ranging from low-fire to stoneware bodies, clear labeling of clay packages is important. Suppliers usually include this identification on both the cardboard carton and the individual plastic bags of clay enclosed. This prevents kiln-firing mishaps that occur when the wrong-formula clay is used.

Dispensing of Raw Materials: For normal use, clay storage in airtight plastic bags appears most practical. The illustration in Fig. 12-4 shows the filling of such bags, each containing 25 pounds. The advantage of this method of storing and using clay is that the clay consistency will remain workable, sometimes for as long as a year. In fact, as often happens, a mold will appear inside the bag. This, to many potters, is a good omen as it indicates that the clay is taking on a desired maturity. Another advantage is the ease of dispensing of clay from these plastic bags. As shown in Fig. 12-5, apportionment of a quantity of clay to a student is handled by peeling down the plastic covering and using a braided wire to skive, or cut off, a portion of clay. One can quickly see that this procedure would lend itself quite well to a group or classroom situation where the dispensing of clay to many pupils might present a difficult problem. If the physical organization of the room is such that it includes rows of tables, a package of clay and a cutoff wire may be placed at the end of each row. The pupils in that row may then pick up or return their clay without creating undue traffic in other areas of the room.

The clay in a plastic-sack arrangement also has a definite advantage in providing a way of returning or saving the unused fresh clay. These clay scraps may be combined at the end of each clay session and placed back into the plastic bag, ready for the next use. The costly process of having metal-lined clay-storage cabinets traditionally associated with damp-clay storage is eliminated.

There are several disadvantages of plastic-bagged clay, however, that should be mentioned. First, prepackaged clay tends to be more expensive than dry clay. Packaged clay also can be restrictive in those situations that call for a highly specialized formulation of a clay body. There is a valuable experience awaiting those pupils who wish to combine their own clay-body ingredients in the development of an individual mixture. One can see that an appreciation and a better understanding of the material will result from this kind of involvement. An assessment should be made, however, concerning the time involved. Could the pupils' time be more valuably spent in such processing of raw materials, or should it be in the designing of the work itself? Some combination of the two might prove the best experience in developing an understanding of the total process.

The Salvage of Material: The reclaiming of scrap clay as shown in Fig. 12-6 can be achieved most satisfactorily, but not without some effort. The usual approach is to wet down the dried clay lumps in a watertight container, such as a plastic garbage can or bucket, and let the mixture stand until all hard clay has absorbed the necessary moisture to become smooth or dissolved. Impurities like plaster particles, wooden sticks and rocks should be kept out of the reclaimed clay. Additional powdered clay, grog or coarse sand may be added to the mixture to bring it back into a desired working consistency (Fig. 12-7).

The Use of Glaze Materials: Glazes present many of the same necessary elements of organization as do the clays. Perhaps the best innovation in dispensing glazes for group instruction is the plastic container. Glass jars sometimes break, with loss of glaze or perhaps injury often resulting. One main difficulty that arises during the glazing procedure is the mixing of glazes during group use.

For example, a brush which is being used for a blue glaze may be carelessly dipped into the white-glaze container. Some method of keying or color-coding of brushes and containers should be considered. It can be particularly confusing because most glaze liquids appear to be in a range between light-gray and black. It can be difficult for pupils even when they use identifying labels, since these often become obscured by glaze drippings. One proved method of control is to limit the glaze of a specific color to a given area of the room. Tying the brush to the glaze container is an extreme precaution, but one that has proven effective in cutting down on glaze mixups.

Handling of Tools and Equipment: The student's own tool box is a consideration that might prove helpful. The box shown in Fig. 12-8 is a fishing tackle box and contains simple tools that are helpful to pupils when working with clay. A shoebox or plastic tote tray will serve well also. Individualized clay-modeling tools are easy to make since they are reasonably simple in design. Students should be encouraged to adapt discarded kitchen tools, such as spoons, for their clay-tooling needs.

Clay-working surfaces may vary. A simple arrangement is to provide each pupil with a piece of rough canvas, much like a placemat. The roughness of this mat is necessary in clay work, as the pupil soon discovers when he finds that wet clay sticks tightly to any smooth surface. A canvas work mat readily releases the clay from its pebbled or rough surface. A canvas covered workboard is a good kind of work-surface arrangement. A particularly good innovation is the clay board. This clay board is completely canvas covered, sewn or tacked on all edges. Waterproof ⅜″ plywood serves as the base. This kind of clay-working surface has several distinct advantages. First, the double sides of these canvas clay boards allow the use of several colors of clay without transfer or staining from a previous work. As an example, one side might be reserved for a red clay and the other side for white, or those clays lacking in oxide stains. Another feature of these clay workboards is that they provide a rigid drying surface that allows a safe transporting surface for clay works. This is particularly useful when pupils work with flat-slab projects where rigid surfaces support the work and limit cracking.

Mounting and Displaying: In displaying three-dimensional clay works, perhaps one of the best methods is to provide each item with a base or, as in the case of a hanging pot, a built-in hanging notch or eyelet in the back of the work. Larger base blocks or stands that do not readily tip over can also save

work from damage (page 94). Smaller sculptural works can be supported with a core pin or shaft. Pupils should be preconditioned early to accept the possibility of project accidents. These do occur often and in many ways—through kiln-firing mishaps, incompatibility of materials, and transportation or display accidents. Growth comes through trial and error and through the pupil's continual design and production of many works. The more the pupil experiments in clay, the less he feels the loss if certain pieces do not develop successfully.

Glossary terms: Blunger, filter press, pug mill.

Fig. 12-2   Crude-clay plaques are inserted into the pugmill mixing chamber, which blends all the clay-body ingredients to an even consistency.

Fig. 12-1   These flat plaques of raw clay will be processed into a blended clay body, suitable for hand building.

Fig. 12-3   The extruded clay is cut away from the pugmill opening after completion of the mixing process. This portion of clay weighs 25 pounds.

Fig. 12-4   A 25-pound cylinder of clay is being packaged in a plastic bag, ready for shipment to studio or classroom.

Fig. 12-5   Wire is used to cut off a portion of clay for a hand-building experience. Dispensing of clay in this manner simplifies the mechanics of group instruction.

Fig. 12-6   Clay scraps should be saved for reprocessing. Here discarded clay is being saved in a plastic tub. Foreign materials like sticks and rocks should be kept out of the scrap-clay storage.

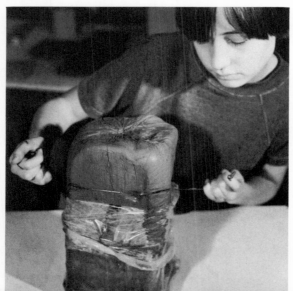

Fig. 12-7 After the clay scraps have been watered down, dissolving takes place and the hard lumps disintegrate. By using two containers grog, dry-clay powder and oxides may be added to the wet clay to bring about a desired consistency.

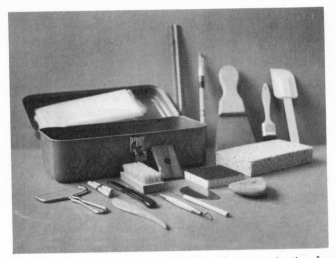

Fig. 12-8 A toolbox is an invaluable aid in organization for clay experiences. A fishing-tackle box or shoebox can be used to hold a variety of items, including tools and cleanup materials. Simple kitchen utensils work very well in most clay processes.

Fig. 12-9 These paddles are valuable shaping and texturing tools. A variety of such tools allows a pupil to develop interesting surface changes.

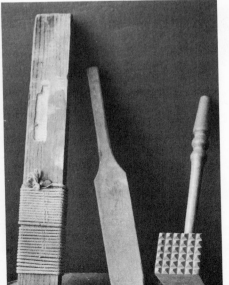

Fig. 12-10 The paddled surface of this box-formed piece was developed with the wooden tenderizer mallet shown on the opposite page.

Fig. 13-1 The grinding wheel is a most efficient tool in the removal of glaze spurs from the bottom of the work.

13. Classroom Safety

In exploring clay techniques and materials, the pupil should observe certain safety precautions. The following suggestions are offered as a guide in meeting unsafe situations that may arise while experimenting with clay.

Clay: As an organic material, clay probably offers as safe a working material as can be found in any art medium. However, clay found in its natural state may contain harmful bacteria and, therefore, should not be consumed internally. This may seem an obvious suggestion, but very young pupils often sample new art materials in such a manner. As an extreme example in the opposite direction, specially processed clays have been known to be purified to the extent that they may be safely used in cosmetics and in a variety of medical applications. This kind of thorough processing is not possible or practical when clay is used in a craft sense.

Each student will have a unique tolerance to a given organic material, so it is possible for some to have reactions to a particular clay makeup or formulation. Specifically, minor skin irritations often do occur when working with heavily grogged and abrasive clays. To minimize such problems, rubber gloves or protective hand lotions are an invaluable classroom and studio aid.

Glaze: Reliable suppliers of ceramic raw materials will usually show the following label on their product if it contains known, potentially toxic ingredients:

> *This is a ceramic material, containing either toxic elements or compounds. Use care in handling. Avoid dust inhalation and prolonged contact with the skin. For use only in the arts of ceramic industries.*

The best approach is to assume that no glaze is entirely nontoxic. This is particularly true for the low-firing, bright-colored glazes such as the oranges and reds. Heavily leaded glazes are potentially harmful in their unfired state and should be handled with care by students. After using liquid glazes, students should be advised to wash their hands thoroughly. Food should not be consumed in the glaze-application area. Among the methods of application, the spraying of glaze is the least desirable in terms of the toxicity factor.

Glaze after Firing: After a glaze has been fired, precautions should be taken to remove carefully all sharp glaze spurs or broken glaze from the bottom of the work. The initial provision of dry-footing or limiting glaze of all work usually prevents the problem of excessive runs of glaze often found around stilts or triangles. If glaze does overrun the bottom of the work during firing, the only effective method of removal is to grind and sand off the protruding surfaces.

Another important consideration is the lead content in glaze used in fired ceramic projects that may serve as food containers. This presents a hazard if the glaze-firing temperature is not high enough, since the lead will still be in a semiraw state. A complete glaze fusing should take place. The makeup of glazes needs to be such that there is a chemical balance that promotes glass forming. Avoidance of low-fire, so-called art, glazes on food containers is perhaps the safest procedure.

Kiln: Unfortunately, the kiln, one of a potter's most valuable pieces of equipment, is often the most abused. The care of the kiln's elements and controls is very important. So is the selection of the safest location in the studio or classroom for the kiln and its proper installation by a competent electrician.

In the operation of a kiln, student mishaps occur

most frequently in the haste of removing articles from the kiln before they have adequately cooled. The temperature or "feel" of items on the top shelf of a finished firing can be misleading: burns can result when the student assumes that the items on the succeeding shelves will be as safe to handle. For classroom use the kiln should receive local fire department inspection service or carry an underwriters' laboratory approval or equivalent.

In most instances, a kiln's location in a classroom or studio should allow at least 12″ between the kiln and walls. A lining or facing of walls around the kiln with transite or asbestos surfacing is recommended. No flammable materials such as paper, rags, plastic, combustible fluids, clothing or cardboard boxes should be stored in the kiln's proximity.

Exhaust of Kiln Fumes: All kilns throw off certain amounts of gasses and excess heat during the firing process. A temperature check of the room or studio should be taken to avoid prolonged temperatures above safe and comfortable levels. Sulfur-dioxide gasses coming out of the kiln during the firing should be allowed some reasonable escape to the outside atmosphere. An open window near the kiln may serve this need.

The positive approach to any multiple kiln installations in crowded or cramped areas is to provide some type of fan-powered exhaust system. This venting is increasingly important when more than one kiln is being fired at the same time.

Rotary Equipment: If a grinder is used in the classroom or studio to finish rough portions of work, goggles should always be worn to protect the eyes of the pupil and those who observe the process. Generally, it is best not to stand close to the grinding operation at any time.

Power hand drills, potter's wheels and other power equipment used in ceramics should be fitted with all necessary safety guards, including eye shields and insulated, grounded wiring. Students need to be instructed in the safe use of all such power equipment before using.

Floors: Water and wet clay left on floors in the studio or classroom may cause falling or slipping. Heavy-textured rubber matting in these areas is recommended.

Plumbing: Particular consideration should be given to classroom or studio plumbing. Preferably, the sink arrangement should have an under-the-sink clay trap that allows the water to pass through but traps the clay particles in a *cul de sac,* or retainer. If a clay trap is not available, then all cleanup of clay tools and washing of hands should be done in a separate container (dishpan or garbage can). The clay, if allowed to settle to the bottom of such a container overnight, leaves the water remaining at the top ready to be skimmed away the next day. The remaining clay can be removed and reprocessed for future use.

Glossary terms: Leaded glaze, glaze spurs, stilts, sulfur dioxide, clay trap.

Fig. 13-2 Excess water and clay tend to separate over a period of several hours. The clay, if allowed to wash down a sink drain, will soon clog the plumbing. It is best to provide clay cleanup containers as a preventive measure.

Glossary

Note: Many of the words below are common in the English language. To avoid confusion, remember that the terms and definitions given here pertain only to the field of ceramics, though any of the given words may have multiple meanings and/or applications.

Adhering Slip—A creamy consistency of liquid clay used as a thin paste to weld individual parts of a clay object together prior to initial firing.

Albany Slip—A brown natural clay slip applied as a glaze medium at high temperatures; used traditionally on bean pots and other similar brown glazed objects, including electrical insulators.

Alkali—A glaze ingredient used to lower the melting level of glazes.

Alkaline Glaze—A glaze formulation that is compounded with frits rather than from raw lead, and is thus considered less toxic.

Applied Clay—Additional clay that is added to the original form for design or decorative purposes.

Applied Relief—A method of surface designing that involves adding clay to the original surface in a raised pattern or design.

Ball Clay—A fine clay added to other clays to produce a clay body that is highly plastic and does not crack when manipulated.

Barium Carbonate—A highly toxic chemical sometimes added to clay by potters to reduce the cloudy or flourlike appearance on the surface of initially fired ware and

sometimes used as flux for earthenware glazes. Note: For classroom purposes the use of this additive would not appear warranted because of its toxicity factor.

Bat—A thick plaster or clay plaque or flat, usually cylindrical, designed to absorb moisture from green or wet clay.

Bell Clapper—The object that strikes the inside of a ceramic bell, causing a sound or ring.

Bisque—A clay object that has had an initial firing only in the kiln—any unglazed ware made ready for glazing.

Blunger—A mechanical device used to break up raw clay while dissolving with water into a clay slip.

Box-Formed Process—Enclosing a rectangular shape with flat-slab sides, top and bottom.

Branch Bottle—A vessel or container with one or more small openings, designed to hold dry weeds or branches decoratively.

Bubbling—Gas eruptions from a clay body that create bubbles or pocked areas in a glazed surface.

Burnishing—The development of a surface finish by stone or hand rubbing. May be applied to unfired, leather-hard clay or to fired clay, as in terra-cotta sculpure.

Carbon 14—A radioactive carbon substance used by archeologists and art historians to determine the dates of inorganic materials, including primitive objects made from fired clay.

Casting Plaster—Basically the same as plaster of paris except for the addition of slow-drying agents, such as glues, that retard the hardening of the plaster.

China Clay—A white clay used in the making of a porcelain clay body.

Chromium Oxide—A colorant used in developing green hues in glaze formulation.

Clay—A combination of alumina silica and water in its pure or natural state, most frequently found combined with other minerals and impurities. It becomes plastic in consistency when water is added and the mixture is manipulated.

Clay Assemblage—The linking together of individual objects into one composition or a grouping of individually composed segments into a central combination that emphasizes the whole as well as highlights separate parts.

Clay-Modeling Tools—Materials, including wire loops with handles, that facilitate the shaping of clay.

Clay Slabs—Rolled, thrown, paddled or pressed clay, producing flat forms with a thickness of ⅜″ to 1″, depending upon the process involved.

Clay Sling—A method of forming which allows suspension of a clay slab in cheesecloth for support. The suspended slab adapts and dries to the sling shape.

Clay Slip—A liquid clay homogenized, or in suspension, primarily poured into molds to produce pottery items.

Clay Strips—Flat clay, cut in long shapes and used in collage construction or as an applied surface decoration element in other projects.

Clay Trap—A device usually attached direcly under a sink facility to hold back liquid clay from plumbing fixtures.

Coil—Long, round or flat strips of clay used in a successive application to build cylindrical enclosed shapes.

Collage—The overlapping of strips or planes of clay that are pressed together to form a flat clay composition.

Colemanite—A borate compound used extensively in glaze formulation and useful in lowering the melting point of a glaze. An excellent glaze base ingredient. (See Surface Design and Decoration)

Coloring Oxides—The clay and glaze-coloring ingredients in stains produced by oxides such as cobalt, copper, iron, nickel and chromium.

Corner Support—A simple corner-supportive device (made from a cardboard box) used to true, or straighten, box shapes made of clay.

Cracking—A structural splitting, usually caused by poor jointing, clay incompatibility or sudden cooling caused by opening the kiln door during firing procedure.

Crazing—A network of fine cracks or fractures formed in glazed surfaces in an overall pattern, usually caused by the stress of firing.

Cross-Tooling—The method of joining edges together in a repetitive tooling and alternating zipper fashion.

Cut Slabs—Clay tiles, cut (usually with a cutoff wire) from a solid clay block to a desired thickness.

Cylindrical Form—A tube or cylinder used as an exterior- or interior-forming device.

De-airing—The squeezing and processing of raw clay through machinery or by hand to enhance its workability.

Dehydration—The process in kiln firing when the clay loses its moisture—between 900°F and 1,100°F. The total lapse of time for this process depends upon the overall kiln load and the thickness of the pieces being fired.

Dipping—Full or partial immersion of an object into a pan or bucket of glaze.

Distortion—Accidental or deliberate misshaping of work during the construction process or firing.

Draped Clay—A clay slab that is lowered into a form or mold to conform to a predetermined shape.

Dry-Footing—The procedure that excludes glaze application from the bottom, or foot, of a work by use of wax or other means. Dry-footing makes kiln stacking more simple, thus eliminating the need for stilts.

Earthenware—A soft red clay requiring low fire; it is usually incapable of being fired over Cone .04 without becoming distorted or melted in the kiln.

Engobes—Decorative liquid clays which are colored by adding oxides and used as underglazes for a color and design medium.

Envelope-Formed Process—Folding slabs of clay to form a closed shape with a minimum of joined edges. Used in constructing informal utilitarian sculptural works.

Epoxy Cement—A highly durable cement that bonds well to ceramics and is frequently colored and used as a filler in cracks or crevasses. Grog or powdered bisque may be blended with it.

Exterior-Formed Process—The pressing of clay into any supporting mold, thus giving the applied clay the shape of the form.

Extruded Clay—Clay which is pushed through the opening of a pugmill to form a specific shape, size and quantity before packaging or direct use.

Filter Press—Clay-processing equipment designed to remove excess moisture from an initial clay mix and to reduce the slip through a cloth-filtering procedure before the mix is placed in the pugmill.

Firebrick—The high-temperature insulation brick used as the kiln's main construction material. Designed to withstand temperatures beyond the kiln's wiring elements' capacity.

Fire Clay—A high-temperature clay usually used in combination with other clays to produce a wide-fire-range clay body.

Firing Range—The maturation span of a clay body or glaze formula—for school use, a span from Cone .06 to Cone 6 is recommended to accommodate the wide range of classroom clay experiences involving varied needs and abilities.

Flat-Slab-Formed Process—Pressing, throwing, rolling, pounding or squeezing clay into a flat shape used in building slab works.

Flux—A ceramic raw material such as colemanite used to cause silica to melt at a lower than normal temperature, thus producing a lower-temperature glaze.

Force-Drying—The drying of a clay object by use of an electric fan or plaster bat, or exposure to warmth.

Fracture—A split in the body form caused by uneven stress or by incomplete joining of the individual parts of a work.

Frit—A finely ground glass or a ground, powdered glaze used in developing particular glaze formulas when combined with other materials, such as clay.

Front-Loading Kiln—A ceramic kiln design which allows stacking and entry to kiln chamber from a front position. The kiln door is usually heavily hung and has a sturdy locking device to keep the door closed during firing.

Glaze Crawling—Glaze which separates into patches rather than remaining in an overall application; frequently found on bisqueware which is oily through excessive handling.

Glaze Dust—Fine particles of dried or sprayed glaze potentially harmful if inhaled or swallowed.

Glaze Opacifiers—A family of oxides such as rutile, tin oxide, zircopax or whiting that are added to transparent or semitransparent glazes to make them milky or opaque.

Glaze Spurs—Sharp, protruding glaze fractures, usually formed when glaze overruns stilts. Spurs may be broken in removal from the work.

Glaze Toxicity—A dangerous factor of glaze ingredients, such as raw lead used as a flux or glaze-melting agent.

Gloss Glaze—A highly reflective glaze (usually applied by brush, dip or spray methods) that produces a glass-like surface.

Greenware—Any item made from clay that has not had an initial firing.

Haniwa—Describes the early Japanese clay shapes, containers or figures, often warriors. These were placed around burial grounds as a means of protection as well as identification.

Grog—A granular mixture of crushed fired-clay particles or other pulverized materials added to clay bodies for strength or for esthetic reasons.

Gum Arabic—A homogenizing agent added to glaze formulas to keep in suspension varied ingredients that have a tendency to separate.

Hand Building—A clay-construction method that relies on nonmechanical means of molding or fabrication as opposed to wheel-thrown or poured processes.

Hand-Formed Process—The manipulating of clay into the cup of one's hand to form a hollow shape, sometimes referred to as a pinch pot.

High Relief—Deep impressions in the clay's surface formed by tool or hand that cause striking changes in the dark-light patterns.

Hip Container—A uniquely designed ceramic flask that is made to conform to and to be carried on the hip. It was developed extensively in Japan.

Interior-Formed Process—The use of a model or shape that permits clay to be applied and conformed to its exterior dimensions.

Iron Oxide—A prime red colorant found in native clays or added to other clays to produce a range of red hues in the matured clay body. Also used as a colorant for glaze, producing browns and tans.

Joining—The gluing or adhering of two clay surfaces together, each initially roughened by tool scratches, with applied clay slip added before pressing and sliding together.

Junior Cone—A small pyrometric shaped cone designed for use in automatic kiln cutoff mechanisms.

Kiln—The heat enclosure used to fire clay. It may be compact and portable (electric) or built in, using gas or wood as the heat-producing fuel.

Kiln Elements—Highly durable nichrome wire-coil heating elements usually imbedded in prepared grooves in the kiln's brick walls.

Kiln Plug—A high-temperature, hollow-ceramic stopper used to close off a peephole in a kiln.

Kiln Posts—High-fired clay-supporting posts used to elevate kiln shelves. They are of various sizes and combinations, depending on the kiln load and sizes of objects being fired.

Kiln-Sitter Cutoff—An added safety device developed for kilns that shuts off electrical power after a predetermined number of hours. It is not controlled by the kiln's inner temperature, as are devices which rely on a cone melting.

Kiln Stacking—The arrangement of a kiln's shelves, stilts, posts and work to accommodate the most items for firing the kiln.

Kiln Wash—A specially compounded high-alumina liquid that is brushed on kiln shelves to prevent adherence of glaze drops or puddles from work being glaze-fired.

Lead Glaze—A glaze formulation that uses raw lead as a melting agent. Bright reds and oranges are often heavily leaded glaze formulas.

Leather-Hard—A term used to define the state of semidryness in an unfired clay object and to indicate a preferred time for final tooling and carving of the clay surface without misshaping or cracking it.

Lead Silicates—A nonwater soluble flux for glaze formulation that is less toxic than red lead oxide.

Low Relief—The delicate shallow incision of a design using line, impressed or carved spaces that lie close to the original surface of a ceramic piece.

Matte Glaze—A low-reflective glaze formulation used extensively where a dull, soft, nonshiny finish is desired. It must be applied with care.

Neriage—The combining of different-colored clays in a layered, pressed-together pattern to accomplish a striking body design. One main clay body is used, but varied in color with oxides to prevent excessive differences in the shrinkage of individual layers (related to procedure used in the collage form process).

Nonfire Glaze—The surface gloss or patina on fired clay produced by grinding, burnishing or any method other than kiln firing.

One-Step Firing—Omission of initial firing before glaze is applied. This practice has an advantage in shortening the time involved, but it also invites project mishaps and kiln failures.

Opaque Glaze—Solid-color glazes that are cloudy in appearance, rather than clear or transparent, and that obscure or cover the original clay-body color.

Pear Pitter—A loop-blade clay tool used to carve and design semidry or leather-hard clay.

Peeling—An incompatibility between glaze and clay body that causes the glaze to curl and pull away from the object's surface.

Peephole—A round opening through the kiln wall, approximately 1″ in diameter, used to inspect the kiln's interior during firing and as a vent opening when left unplugged during firing.

Pinch Pot—A simple bowl-forming method that utilizes the hands only by cupping and pressing into the clay simultaneously to form a hollow shape.

Plaster Bat—A cast plaster shape, usually round and from ¾″ to 2″ thick, used to increase moisture absorption from the clay to the plaster.

Plaster Mold—A moisture-absorbing exterior-form enclosure made from plaster of paris and used to reproduce a single clay shape in quantity.

Plaster of paris—A gypsum compound in powder form that is quickly formed into solid material after being mixed with water.

Porcelain—An extremely high-fire clay body maturing at Cone 10 and above, and resulting in the most vitreous of all high-fire ceramic ware.

Porosity—The inherent graininess or open quality of a clay body designed to withstand the stress of drying and firing without undue warping and shrinkage that are inherent with ungrogged clay. The addition of grog increases the openness of the clay. The lack of grog results in a tighter clay body, along with an increased shrinkage factor.

Pressed Relief—The result of pressing into clay with a variety of objects that are designed to create impressions, as opposed to using the original flat-surface levels.

Prestiffened—A curing, or drying, of the wet clay before assembling or cutting.

Pugmill—A mechanical mixing machine which manipulates dry and wet clays including other clay-body ingredients such as grog to a working plastic consistency.

Pyrometer—An exterior gauge serving as a supplementary kiln-heat-indicating device, connected to the kiln's interior by a twin-wire heat-measuring unit called a thermocouple.

Raku Ware—Pottery made from a highly grogged clay body designed for a glaze-firing method that results in quick cooling and produces high color and textural changes.

Raw Clay—Clay found in its natural state with nothing added or changed; it is later processed and made plastic and workable.

Red Lead Oxide—A highly poisonous water-soluble fluxing ingredient. Red lead oxide is not recommended in glaze formulations intended for student use.

Refractory Brick—A light-colored insulating brick commonly used in kiln construction and designed to withstand extremely high temperatures.

Relief Design—The three-dimensional surface treatment of a piece with a carved or applied clay design, or a combination of both.

Rolled Slabs—Flat clay cakes or plaques flattened to a uniform thickness with a rolling pin or any sturdy tubular shape.

Sagging—A bending or distortion of a clay shape produced during either the forming or firing processes.

Sgraffito (or graffito)—A method of surface designing in clay and glaze that utilizes a scratched line to expose the background color or to incise a legend.

Sculptural—A characteristic quality of the clay-working method that emphasizes a modeled appearance.

Senior Cone—A large pyrometric cone designed for use in kilns that use a sight or manual method of kiln shut-off.

Slab-Coil-Formed Process—The construction of cylindrical shapes by adding succeeding lengths of coils, either slabbed or rolled.

Slip Trailer—A syringe, eye dropper, simple wax-paper sheet or other tool used for applying clay slip to produce a relief line design.

Slumping—The sagging of wet clay during processing, or the bending or distortion of clay caused by overfiring.

Silica—One of the basic ingredients in kiln wash, acting as a protective surface coating applied to kiln shelves but destructive to kiln-wiring elements if accidentally brushed or dripped on them during kiln applications. Also, the glass-forming agent in glaze.

Shrinkage—The dehydration of the plastic clay, which varies with the composition of the clay body and grog content. A range of 5 to 20% shrinkage may be expected among different combinations of clays.

Smooth Clay—A clay body that is relatively devoid of grog in its natural state or has been cleansed by processing through a fine mesh screen to remove inherent grog ingredients. (Primarily recommended for wheel-throwing.) Avoiding rough surface textures aids those with skin irritations.

Stoneware Clay—A high-fire clay body that readily withstands firing temperatures to Cone 6 or higher, but is earthenware at lower temperatures, such as Cone .06.

Sulfur Dioxide—A nonflammable pungent gas produced as a waste or byproduct during the kiln-firing process. It may produce an unpleasant atmosphere if large amounts are present.

Sparse Glazing—The practice of minimizing the glaze application to emphasize the natural clay body.

Spatter Technique—A random application of glaze, engobes or wax-resist usually achieved through a flipping action with a glaze-loaded brush.

Slip Trailing—A process involving the use of slip, slightly thickened, trailed with a squeeze bottle or small syringe directly onto greenware.

Stamping—A method used to impress into damp clay a design previously tooled into a clay or plaster stamping tool.

Stilts—Kiln furniture designed to elevate objects to be glazed-fired above the kiln-shelf surface and designed in a triangular shape with three peaks for minimum contact with glazed surfaces.

Stitching—A method of joining clay slabs together by alternating tool impressions from one wall to another in much the same manner as in stitching or cross-hatching.

Tape Resist—A technique of applying masking tape to bare bisque or to a glazed surface prior to final glaze application and firing. The tape burns away, and the surface beneath contrasts with the glazed surface.

Template—A paper or cardboard outline shape that is laid over a clay slab to outline roughly the total or individual parts of work.

Temporary Molds—One-of-a-kind supportive devices made of paper, cardboard, cork or other similar materials, as opposed to plaster molds, which are intended for multiple production.

Terra-Cotta—Described in history as "baked earth." A low- to moderate-fire, rather soft, ceramic clay body ranging in a maturation color from light pink, to rust, to dull orange, heavily grogged, particularly suited for sculpture. Terra-cotta is quite porous, and therefore usually incapable of holding liquids.

Test Tiles—Sampler slabs prepared to illustrate textural and glaze techniques.

Trailing—The application of glaze, slip, engobes or wax-resist mediums in a line design.

Transferring—The process of moving delicate works to be fired to the kiln. Also used to designate a pattern or design that will be transferred from a template to the material.

Translucent Glaze—Glaze that allows an undercolor to show through, usually offering a high-gloss surface quality.

Throwing—Formation of a ceramic pot on the potter's wheel either electrically powered or manually turned. Also, the formation of a flat clay slab by hand.

Thrown Slabs—Flat slabs produced by throwing a quantity of clay onto a work surface in a swinging motion designed to spread and flatten the clay with each successive throw.

Tool Marks—Impressions made by hand or tool and left purposely on a clay object as part of the surface textural design.

Tooled Relief—A process of carving into the clay's surface to develop a relief or interior design or pattern.

Top-Loading Kiln—A ceramic kiln with the chamber opening from the top, allowing entry and loading from above. The kiln door is kept closed by gravity and does not require latching.

Toxicity Factor—The degree to which a given material or

element of a material may be poisonous or otherwise injurious to health.

Undercuts—Surface details or any parts of the original mold design that trap applied clay and prevent its removal.

Underglaze—The initial application of surface decoration in engobe, glaze or stain.

Vitrification—The nonporous stage of maturity in firing that causes the clay body to become closed and impervious to moisture or liquid.

Warpage—The bending or misshaping of a fired clay often caused by too little inherent grog or a too-intense drying or firing cycle.

Watertightness—The ability of a container to hold liquids as a result of its complete interior glazing.

Wax-Resist—The application of wax, either in liquid form or crayon, to an initially fired clay surface. It may be applied over a glaze before the final glaze is added to produce an undercolor pattern or design.

Wax-Resist Medium—Any wax material such as crayon, pencil or paraffin, which can be heated to a fluid state; or specially prepared water-soluble wax solutions, designed to resist glazes after drying.

Wedging—The process of hand manipulation of clay to remove air pockets and to develop the raw clay body into a working consistency with plasticity.

Weld Marks—The tooling and joining of separate clay parts by pressing an alternating, or locking, pattern along the adjoining seams.

Wind Bell—A ceramic bell, designed to function in much the same manner as metal bells but with a different, a distinctive ring.

Zircopax—A glaze additive used in making transparent glazes more opaque.

Acknowledgments

The author wishes to express his deep sense of appreciation for the interest and cooperation shown by the many imaginative artist-craftsmen, both professional and nonprofessional, who permitted their work to be photographed and incorporated into this book.

From Finland, long a leading country in the design of quality crafts, came examples produced by such artists as Rut-Bryk, Annikki Hovisari, Taesto Kaasinen, Birger Kaipianen, Francesca Lindh and Oiva Toikka. These Finnish artists have brought fame to their native country at international exhibitions including the Milan Triennales, where they have taken a total of four Grand Prix, six Gold Medals, four Silver Medals and seven Diplomas d'Honore.

Japan is currently perhaps the most productive nation in terms of the potter's craft; Mutsuo Yanigihara, an internationally known artist, particularly in the area of surface texture and glaze decoration, has provided valuable assistance.

Artist-craftsmen from the United States also generously consented to include examples of their work. Illustrations were collected from such well-known American craftsmen as Rudy Autio from Montana; Edward Traynor, potter-educator from the University of California at Los Angeles; Ralph and Lorene Spencer, master potters of Seattle; and Robert Sperry, potter-educator from the University of Washington. Others included are Dave Shaner, potter with the Archie Bray Foundation in Montana; Bob James, faculty member of the school of art at the University of Oregon; John Fassbinder, sculptor from Claremont, California; Larry Zion, Highline College faculty; Phillip Levine, a Seattle sculptor; and Wendy Trosper, a Northwest potter. Talented students whose individual efforts are featured include Jerry Baldwin, Candy Coffelt, Donna Lawrence and James Stipes.

The author is grateful for photographs and valuable technical assistance concerning kilns and kiln temperatures and related processes which were received from the Edward Orton Jr. Ceramic Foundation in Columbus, Ohio; from Skutt and Sons, Inc., in Portland, Oregon; from the Spencer Pottery in Seattle, Washington; from the Interpace Corporation in Los Angeles, California; and from the Arabia Corporation in Helsinki, Finland.

The Seattle Art Museum generously provided photographs of its extensive collection of ceramic works of the past for part of the historical material. The author acknowledges, in particular, Dr. Richard Fuller, Director, and Dorothy Lahr, Director of Education, of the Seattle Art Museum. Audrianna Allen provided excellent suggestions in the organization and sequence of the written material. A special thanks is also given to the author's students, who, though they may not have been acknowledged individually here, developed many of the unique clay-working approaches that were shared in this book.